Kernels of Truth

Volume 2
The Kingdom, Prodigals, And Happiness

By Larry Grainger
Foreword by Bob Mumford

Table of Contents

Foreword

Larry has a unique gift of illuminating truth in the Word of God and showing us how to actually apply it to everyday life. Among many essential topics, it asks and answers the timeless question, "Why am I here?" These kernels of truth are vital in the present season of change.

Through these writings not only does Larry show us how to mature spiritually and relationally, he also shows us the importance of being God's representatives in the earth. He masterfully shows us that only through an intimate relationship with our Creator can we learn to reflect God's glory.

Kernels of Truth: The Kingdom, Prodigals and Happiness is a rich compilation of biblically based truths that will change your life. They shed new light and challenge you to rethink old paradigms. Larry's progression through understanding what the Kingdom of God is like to discerning between God's wishes and desires, to the true meaning of happiness is seamless. And, as if that isn't enough, his insight into celebrating Life and Light makes this book a must read. It is one of the few that truly reflects God's glory.

Bob Mumford
September 1, 2009

Introduction

Near the end of 1998, I felt the Lord impressing upon me to begin to write a teaching newsletter that would focus on a simple handling of the Scripture in such a way that it would meet us where we live. I had no idea how I would proceed, nor if anyone would even care to read what I would write.

Always believing the best way to begin a venture is to just start, I commenced in January of 1999 to write this monthly newsletter which I felt should be called the Kernels of Truth. After submitting it to the local pastor at the time, I then proceeded to publish the first issue in February of 1999.

To my amazement, as I published the letter each month, numerous people began to share with me that not only were they reading the Kernels, but were actually enjoying and being blessed by it. I am still almost giddy when, after over 10 years of publishing the newsletter, someone tells me they really look forward to the mailing each month.

Some time ago, people began to suggest that I should release the Kernels of Truth in book form and make it available on a broader scale. In February 2009 we released the first volume which included all the newsletters from the year 1999.

This second volume is the collection of Kernels of Truth written in the year 2000. I trust both volumes will inspire and assist you in your walk with Jesus Christ.

As of the writing of this introduction, the Kernels of Truth currently goes to approximately 200 addresses, including two gentlemen in prison and one reader in northern Canada. I only wonder what the Lord will do with the future of the newsletter and how long He would have me to continue write it. But for now, I trust you will enjoy this installment of the second year's issues of the Kernels of Truth.

Why Are You Here?

Demetrius, the silversmith, was growing increasingly disturbed concerning the message that Paul the apostle was spreading around. "How dare he diminish the value of our man-made gods? Someone has got to do something about this busybody," he thought, "and it may as well be me." He called the other silversmiths together and began to speak to them with the intended purpose of creating a disturbance that would drive Paul out of Ephesus. "Friends, you know that we make a good living at this. But you have surely seen and heard how this man Paul is upsetting a lot of people, not only in Ephesus, but almost everywhere in Asia. He claims that the gods we humans make are not really gods at all. Everyone will start saying terrible things about our business. They will stop respecting the temple of the goddess Artemis, who is worshiped in Asia and all over the world. Our great goddess will be forgotten!" Does it seem awfully convenient to you that defending the false goddess and her reputation was directly beneficial to their moneybags? I don't think they were as concerned with the promotion of the religion of the day as they were perpetuating their cash cow. If an image of Yahweh would have lined their pockets, Demetrius and his gang would have been inviting Paul over for some kosher Gentile supper.

Well, the crowd really responded when their lady god was seemingly impugned. A mild riot ensued and they seized a couple of Paul's traveling companions and assembled in the theatre. Paul, in his usual feisty manner, wanted to appear before the crowd and confront them, but the disciples that were with him restrained him from entering. Then, Luke writes a most interesting line in Acts chapter 19, verse 32. Upon reading this verse one time, a phrase I had read many times literally jumped off the page at me. I have it underlined in my bible. "The assembly was in confusion: Some were shouting one thing, some another. ***Most of the people did not even know why they were there***." Well, logic and sensibility resolved the situation in the theatre, but my focus is on this line.

It is important that we not be drawn into a place where we do not even know why we are present. A clear purpose and vision is most valuable in keeping us out of the "theatre of confusion." Do you know why you are here? Allow me to illuminate some things that are a part of **not** knowing why we are here or "there" as it may be.

1. To begin with, the most obvious is a state of **confusion**. If we are just following the crowd

without a strong sense of convictions, we are bound to a state of confusion when confronted with reality. Some things sound really nice and spiritual, but when faced with actual life circumstances, we will be confused as to why things didn't turn out the way we thought they would. 2. Along with confusion, we tend to be **gullible** to most anything if we don't have a strong sense of why we are here. It's the old adage, "If you believe in nothing, you will fall for anything." Or, as the Lord God declared to Isaiah in the 7th chapter and 9th verse of his book, *"If you do not stand firm in your faith, you will not stand at all."* I'm sure there were people in that crowd who went along because they had no good reason to do otherwise, even though they may not have had strong feelings about the idol making industry. 3. A third trap we can fall into without clear definition of why we are here is one of **rationalization**. Rationalization is the molding of an argument to fit our own personal agenda. Rationalization is fooling ourselves into thinking we care about the "reputation of Artemis" so we can perpetuate our own idol-making trade. 4. And, closely related, if we have no clue as to why we are here, we are given to **self-preservation** and **a self-serving agenda**. If we cannot see anything outside of our own world, we will definitely be consumed with our own desires and aspirations. Demetrius couldn't see anything else outside his own agenda and had no room for another message. We will always be forced to get outside ourselves and find out why we are here.

As I write these words (in December) we are facing a New Year. Whether you believe the new millennium starts on January 1, 2000, or 2001, there is something distinctively different from 1999 and 2000. By the time you read this, we will all know the impact of the Y2K situation, whether it is a major impact on our lives or just an insignificant nuisance. But regardless of that dynamic, there is another dynamic involved here. There seems to be a fresh sense, in the Spirit, of a season of change and new beginnings as we enter into the year 2000. I have never considered myself to be a prophet, and still don't, but I can sense that this is a real time of inventory and re-assessment on our part. One of the things we must ask ourselves is "*Why Am I Here?*" Where is here? Due to the limited space of this newsletter, I will deal with two "heres."

The first is why are you here on this *earth*? Are you just a blob of plasma that God gave life to so you could occupy a few square inches at any given time? Is the entirety of your life to be born, go to school, get a job, retire and then die? I think not. Some people, and, in all likelihood, someone reading this newsletter, think they are somewhat of an accident conceived in a time of passion and somehow God just puts up with them because, after all, He is a loving God. He is a loving God, and because He is motivated by love, He has chosen to give you and me life. Deuteronomy 32:39 says, "*See now that I myself am He! There is no god besides me. I put to death and I bring to life . . .*" We must understand we are in the hands of the Giver of life and if He has breathed life into us, He has a higher purpose for us than just to maintain a spot on this terrestrial ball. The Great Creator was involved in your life long before that mean doctor whacked you on your little bottom. Look what David declared in Psalm 139:13-16, "*For you created my inmost being; **you knit me together in my mother's womb**. I praise you because I am **fearfully and wonderfully made**; your works are wonderful, I know that full well. My frame was **not hidden** from you when I was made in the secret place. When I was woven together in the depths of the earth, **your eyes saw my unformed body. All the days ordained for me were written in your book before one of them came to be**.*" What the psalmist writes here is not David specific. What was true about David is just as true about you and me. Know this, all **your** days were written in His book before you lived the first one. So, why am I here on this circle that hangs in the vast expanse we call space? Consider this. God made mankind in His image, with innate characteristics that are God-like. He then proclaimed that mankind should ". . . *rule over the* fish of the sea and birds of the air, over the livestock, over all the earth, and over all the creatures that move along the ground." Again, in Psalm 8:6, "You made him ruler over the works of your hands; you put everything under his feet." We are stewards over God's creation and His representatives in the earth of the Godhead. We have the responsibility to demonstrate His goodness in the earth through our relationship with Him, our Maker. Why are you here? You exist to reveal His glory to your fellow man, and thus call all people back to a relationship with their Creator. Let's look at two Scriptures. First, look at Isaiah 6:3. "And they were calling to one another: 'Holy, holy, holy is the Lord Almighty; the whole earth is filled with his glory.' " It is an established fact that the earth is filled with the glory of the Lord. This is an eternal truth that is unalterable because the earth and everything it contains is the Lord's. While the earth is full of God's glory, it is obviously **not** filled with the **knowledge** of His glory. In the second Scripture, Habakkuk 2:14, the prophet proclaims, "For the earth **will be filled** with the **knowledge** of the glory of the Lord, as the waters cover the sea." Here is where the reason why we are here comes in. The translators of the Contemporary English Version of the Bible worded it this way, "Just as the water fills the sea, the land will be filled with **people** who know and honor the Lord." It falls on us, God's people, to so honor the Lord, that people will become acquainted with the glory of our God. What is His glory? As an old time charismatic, I have thought at times that God's glory was some kind of cloud, or an outbreak of miracles, or some other fantastic occurrence. While I am all for these events taking place, I think I am beginning to come into a clearer idea of just what God's glory really is. While recently listening to two teaching series, one by Brother Charles Simpson and one by Brother Bob Mumford, I was able to see how God described His glory to Moses. Look at Exodus 33. In verse 18, Moses asks God to let him see His glory. The Lord's reply was this. *"I will cause all my goodness to pass in front of you, and I will proclaim my name, the Lord, in your presence. I will have mercy on whom I will have mercy, and I will have compassion on whom I will have compassion."* In response to Moses' request for God to show him His glory, God replies that He will show Moses His goodness and mercy. This gives us a glimpse of what it is that we are to demonstrate in the earth. In verses 5 and 6 of chapter 34, He further describes the characteristics we are to reveal to our fellow man. *"The LORD descended in the cloud and stood there with him as he called upon the name of the LORD. Then the LORD passed by in front of him and proclaimed, The LORD, the LORD God, compassionate and gracious, slow to anger, and abounding in lovingkindness and truth; who keeps lovingkindness for thousands, who forgives iniquity, transgression and sin.*" I will resist the urge to expound on this passage further, but will rather list what I think is the glory of God that He wants us to reveal in the earth. The Lord sums up His glory as His goodness and mercy. Then, as He passes in front of Moses, He identifies the qualities that go along with His glory. I'll not comment on these individually, but rather just list them.

1. Compassion   Zechariah 7:9, Colossians 3:12
2. Graciousness or full of grace.   I Peter 4:10
3. Slowness to anger.   James 1:19-21
4. Abounding in mercy   Luke 6:36-38
5. Truthful or faithful   III John 4
6. Covenant faithfulness   Proverbs 18:24
7. Forgiveness   Matthew 6:14-15

These are the "communicable attributes" of God and they illustrate how God wants to be revealed in the earth. There are characteristics that the Father never intended us to totally see or have the ability to reveal, (My face must not be seen), but these attributes are our responsibility to reveal in our realm as Christ is formed in us. (Galatians 4:19) Why are you here? You are here primarily to reveal the glory of God in the earth for all creation to see. Romans 8:29, "*For those whom He foreknew, He also predestined to become conformed to the image of His*

Son, so that He would be the firstborn among many brethren;"

The second "here" I want to deal with is, why are you here in the _church_? Because I believe our involvement in the local church exhibits our involvement in the church at-large, why are you "here" or "there"? We must ask ourselves this question with a sincere heart. Now, first let me qualify that a local body doesn't always have to be a building with a steeple on it. There are many variations of what constitutes a local church, and for further instruction on that, please read the previous volume of Kernels of Truth. In whatever variety of local spiritual family you find yourself, are you there because your grandmother was there, and it is the only thing you have ever known? Could it be because you like the music that is presented in the corporate meetings? Or, maybe it is the youth programs that are offered? Is that the reason that you are "here"? Let me ask another question. Do you attend church on Sunday morning to be entertained and yet refrain from being an active part of the body the rest of the week? Why are you here? There is one question to ask yourself that will determine your motivation for being in the church or fellowship of which you call yourself a part. *Am I "here" because this is where the Lord God Almighty has placed me?* Great music is wonderful; enlightening youth and children programs are very attractive, as they should be; even inspiring preaching and teaching is necessary to keep our attention. But, the bottom line we must ask ourselves is, "has God adopted me into this spiritual family?" For, you see, if we can answer an affirmative to this question, and I believe most of us can, it will change how we relate to the local body. Here, at the beginning of another year, ask yourself these questions. Resolve to have clarity about your role in the church, and, if you need help, seek out the leadership or a friend who can help you with your search. Determine not to be a fringe part of the living organism we call the church. Jesus said "the poor we will always have with us," (he wasn't just speaking monetarily), but you don't have to be one of the spiritually deficient ones. The most important thing isn't what you do, but the resolution of this question. Why am I here? The proper answer will take care of our doing what we need to do.

The flip side of that is, if it is truly God who has placed us in the local body, shouldn't it be Him who removes us from the local body? Here is where people have problems. When the pastor or elders make us mad, we want to change addresses or "move my letter." When there isn't enough excitement to suit us, we have a tendency to wander around looking for the nearest spiritual circus. And, when we begin to feel that God may be crowding us, and using some of His kids to do it, we will definitely feel led to find another place to worship. What would happen if we remained where we were even in these circumstances because we were aware that it was He who placed us and we were only going to let *Him* "un-place" us? Is it possible that some, under the reading of my thoughts, have habitually moved around every time God got frighteningly close to performing some operation on our character or thought process? If we have a firm conviction concerning why we are here, it gives God the liberty to make any adjustments to us He deems necessary without the danger of our removing ourselves. Paul wrote to the church at Philippi, ". . . *being confident of this, that he who **began a good work** in you **will carry it on to completion** until the day of Christ Jesus.*" The Father will not give up on us no matter how long it takes; but, our being clear on why we are here will allow us to cooperate with His workings and, just maybe, speed up the process. If you have been a wanderer, never putting down roots anywhere, allow me to encourage you; it is time to make a change. Ask the question, and then, allow God to plant you in the soil of your answer. Why are you here?

Maybe this will stimulate you to inventory other areas of your life. Why are you in the vocation in which you find yourself? Allow me to repeat that most people in the church are called to some type of vocation. It is not just what we do to make a living. Why are you in that relationship? Why are you about to marry that man or woman? Answers to these questions and others will stabilize your life in ways you aren't aware.

Most of the people did not even know why they were there.

The Kingdom of God is Like

W hile teaching the disciples how to pray and what foundational issues they should keep before God, Jesus prayed this prayer. *"Thy kingdom come, Thy will be done, on earth as it is in heaven."* The kingdom of God is somewhat of an anomaly to our western civilization mode of thinking. We are not too familiar with kings; thus the concept of a kingdom is one to which we must adjust. Nevertheless, I can assure you there is much more in the Scripture about kingdoms, kings and princes than presidents, congressmen and senators. While this is not a political forum, and will remain thus, I will point out that we err when we attempt to govern the church in the same manner as our nation governs itself. We should learn from the written lessons given us rather than emulating a secular form of government. And those written lessons are chock-full of references to our God and Lord being a king and reigning over His kingdom. It would do you well to get your concordance and look up every occurrence of the word "kingdom;" I will only refer to a few. Psalm 22:28 – *"The kingdom is the Lord's, and He rules over the nations."* Psalm 145:13 – *"Your* kingdom is an everlasting kingdom, and Your dominion endures throughout all generations." Matthew 6:32-33, "For all these things the Gentiles eagerly seek; for your heavenly Father knows that you need all these things. But **seek first His kingdom** and His righteousness; and all these things shall be added to you." Matthew 4:23 – "And Jesus was going about in all Galilee, teaching in their synagogues, and proclaiming the good news of the kingdom, and healing every kind of disease and every kind of sickness among the people." This good news of the kingdom that Jesus preached is about the existence of a Kingdom where all who turn to Him may know God's good government. The kingdom of God is God's government established under the rulership of His Son, Jesus Christ, and administered in the earth by the church. The reign of Jesus over the Kingdom produces order, righteousness, peace and joy in the Holy Spirit. In praying "thy kingdom come, thy will be done, on earth as it is in heaven," Jesus was teaching the disciples that the Kingdom had not only future, but also, present implications. A kingdom is the territory or inhabitants that are subject to a king. With that established, it is elementary to comprehend how God's kingdom is a present reality that influences and affects our everyday life. It is important for us to assess our relationship with the King, and make sure that we don't view Him as some spiritual Santa Claus, but rather as our Sovereign One; our Potentate; the Captain of the Lord's host. (see Joshua 5:13)

Allow me at this point to give an unsolicited plug. The brevity of this newsletter will prevent me from even scratching the surface concerning the subject of the kingdom of God. One of the best study tools available today, which not only covers the issues of the kingdom of God, but the whole spectrum of our Christian life, is the book *The Covenant and the Kingdom* by Charles Simpson. If you do not already have a copy of this work, let me encourage you to get one. It is arranged in such a manner as it can be used as a daily devotional or a tool for a Bible study. You can go to http://www.csmpublishing.org and order your copy there. You will thank me for this recommendation.

Daniel was called in to stand before King Nebuchadnezzar to not only interpret his dream, but to first tell him *what* he had dreamed. The king had seen a large statue which had a head of gold, its breast and its arms were silver, its belly and thighs were bronze, its legs were made of iron, and its feet were made up partly of iron and clay. He then saw a stone that crushed the statue starting with the feet and working its way up the head. Daniel interpreted the dream to mean each of the layers was a different kingdom and the stone was the ultimate kingdom. In verse 38 of chapter 2, King

Nebuchadnezzar heard Daniel say, "You are the head of gold." The sermon was over as far as old Nebuchadnezzar was concerned, for, in his mind, he started designing the image of gold chapter 3 records. But what Daniel went on to say was this; *"And in the days of those kings the God of heaven will set up a kingdom which will never be destroyed, and that kingdom will not be left for another people; it will crush and put an end to all these kingdoms, but it will itself endure forever."* Obviously, that kingdom is the kingdom of God and His Son, Jesus Christ. We don't have to read the back of the book to see who wins; we find it right here in Daniel. You should continue reading Daniel, as there are several references to the victorious kingdom and the part we have.

One of the things we find is that Jesus, while on the earth, spent a tremendous amount of time teaching about the kingdom of God. In most cases he used parables to instruct the disciples and others about this mystery. Usually, He would start His parable by saying, "The kingdom of God is like..." thus, the title of this newsletter. I want to examine a few of the parables and try to pull some principles from them that may help us to identify and be good citizens of this heavenly kingdom which is being established on earth. I must admit that I don't feel I have even begun to touch all that Jesus was trying to convey with His parables, but I do think we can find a few simple lessons that will help us in this endeavor we call life.

The <u>parable of the sower and the soil</u> is recorded in three gospels. Matthew 13:1-23, Mark 4:1-20, and Luke 8:4-10. I trust you will read these passages, as I do not have the space to cover them here. Here are some things we learn from this story. **1.** *Understanding and comprehending the kingdom requires hearing ears and seeing eyes.* Solomon declared in Proverbs 20:12 that *"the hearing ear and the seeing eye, the Lord has made both of them."* The natural mind or intellect can never comprehend the mysteries of the Kingdom of God. We are required to have a living, active, personal relationship with the Lord if we are ever to grasp the truth about His domain in our lives. Notice verses 14-17 of Matthew 13. Many people still today try to understand this mysterious kingdom with its backwards and upside down principles, but the only avenue to understanding is through ears that hear the master's voice and spiritual eyes that are able to view the truth of the Spirit. **2.** *We must embrace the word God gives us or Satan will steal it.* Remember, he is after the seed. (Luke 8:11) John 8:37 *"I know you are Abraham's descendants. Yet you are ready to kill me, because you have <u>no room</u> for my word."* Sometimes the thing that keeps us from being the good ground is that we haven't truly embraced the word to us from

God. Look at the definition of embrace and think of it in terms of the word of God. **Embrace = To fasten on as armor; To seize eagerly.** There is a difference between believing the word of God is true and latching on to it like it was our last breath of air. We must embrace it. **3.** *We must submit to the process of God so He can break up our fallow or unplowed ground (Jeremiah 4:3) and give us depth to receive the word.* If we habitually contend with the process of God, we will not be good receptacles for the word God desires to reveal to us and in us. It is the dealings of God that prepare our hearts for the planting of His seed in our lives. The biggest enemy to this process is isolation. We need brothers and sisters to be around us when we are feeling squeezed by our circumstances. Peter writes in his first letter that we shouldn't be caught off guard at the fiery ordeal that comes upon us for our testing, as though some strange thing was happening to us. The process of pressure God takes us through is not strange at all, but the tool he uses to form the nature and character of Christ in our lives. **4.** *We must be free of alternate concerns and interests that war against the word.* Wow, I could dedicate a whole newsletter to this one subject. Busyness, clutter, distractions, agendas, schedules, and many other things like these can choke the word. We must be able to properly manage our lives and not let our life manage us. We should determine what is priority and what is not, and make adjustments accordingly. In addition, it behooves us to identify those concerns and activities that conflict with the word in us and find a way to sever the ties to these also. **5.** *An honest and good heart is the proper vessel for the word of God.* People of good ground hold fast to the word with all perseverance.

The parable of the <u>treasure and the pearl</u> is recorded in Matthew 13:44-46. We are able to draw one major application from this parable. *We must sell out to realize the full benefits and impact of the Kingdom.* King Solomon recorded in the 23rd Proverb and verse 23 *"Buy the truth and do not sell it."* We must make the decision that the pearl and treasure we have found is not worth any exchange, regardless of the rate of currency might be. Once we find the truth, it must never be on the selling block. One of the things that deeply saddens me, (and I believe also the Lord - See Revelation 3:15-16) is the practice of casual Christianity. A half-hearted approach to the kingdom of God may as well be a no-hearted approach. Our great country is probably the most vulnerable to this degeneration, because of our prosperity as a nation and our lifestyle of comfort. While I am not opposed to comfort, I am opposed to the seemingly nonchalant attitude I find among some church people and their "it doesn't really matter" approach to citizenship in the ultimate kingdom. Jesus declared that this kingdom is "forcibly entered" and "violent men take it by force." There is no place for casualness in either of those descriptions. Let us seize the treasure we have found, realizing the value of what we have been given.

The parable of the growing seed is found in Mark 4:26-29. In this parable, Jesus teaches us about productivity in and by the kingdom. There are four points that I think we should deal with. **1.** *All productivity in the kingdom begins with the sowing of a seed.* It is a natural phenomenon that the Creator put into place. The Lord promised to Noah that "*While the earth remains, seedtime and harvest, and cold and heat, and summer and winter, and day and night shall not cease.*" Genesis 8:22. The sowing and reaping of seed is just as much a natural law as summer and winter or cold and heat. The lesson to be learned here is that when God puts something into our hands, we are expected to recognize some of it as seed and to plant it into good soil. Whatever God has given you, be willing to part with some of it and you will begin the process of being productive in the kingdom. **2.** *We don't need to understand how the seed grows----just that it does.* We must grasp the idea that it is God who gives the increase, and we are only the planters. Paul attempted to communicate this to the church in Corinth when he said, "*I planted, Apollos watered, but it was God who was causing the* *growth.*" I Corinthians 3:6. We do not need to be seed inspectors. But we are simply instructed to obey God and let Him be responsible for the maturation of the seed. **3.** *Growth is a natural progression of stages.* Our American expediency causes us to want to take shortcuts to purpose. "Lord give me patience . . . and I want it now!" Have you ever known someone who prayed that prayer or one like it? Maybe it was you. We want to get from point "a" to point "z" in 15 seconds and the Lord wants us to learn that "b" through "y" are necessary steps to be mature, contributing citizens of the kingdom. The same God who created the natural seasons wants to take you and me through seasons of growth. This takes time and requires trust and obedience on our part. **4.** *All mature fruit is to be harvested.* This is another natural law that cannot be altered. If we don't harvest that mature apple from the tree, it will fall to the ground anyway. God expects to harvest the results of His planting in us by receiving some talent or gift to be used for His purpose in the earth. God does not give us seed to produce solely for our own consumption, but rather, to be participants in supplying to the kingdom of which we are constituents.

The parable of the mustard seed and yeast is found in Matthew 13:31-33; Mark 4:30-32; and Luke 13:18-19. We find one huge lesson in this parable. *The kingdom of God, though seemingly insignificant, will covertly "leaven" the whole society on earth.* Just as the lady hid the leaven in the meal, God has hidden His kingdom inside another society, with the ultimate purpose of permeating it with the glory of His kingdom. Yes, there are public demonstrations of the kingdom through newspaper and television. But the real effectiveness is taking place at the grass roots level in a covert fashion. One on one and small group relationships are the very essence of what Jesus established while on the earth and teaching the disciples how to conduct themselves. Thank God for the results of large meetings and television shows, as a great host of people have been converted through these mediums. But the real growth of the kingdom takes place as you and I relate to one another and the lost people He puts in our path. This ultimate kingdom will indeed be larger than all the other plants and it is a place of rest and sanctuary.

The parable of the workers in the vineyard is recorded in Matthew 20:1-16. The first lesson I see here is a crucial one. **1**. *It's **His** Kingdom.* If we will settle that issue, we will find all the other ones easier to grasp. The kingdom of God is not a democracy. He isn't interested in our vote. He is the King of kings and we are His subjects. We have to believe that "Father Knows Best." **2**. Closely related to that, *we must understand it is the king's* *prerogative to pay whomever and whatever he wishes.* We sometimes don't understand why He would bless old brother so and so and we seemingly are left standing in need. I don't have all the answers to those type of questions (as a matter of fact, I have very few) but one thing we must understand. We can not allow ourselves to make an issue of what He does or does not pass on to us or anyone else. We should rejoice at the blessing of our brother or sister rather than allow jealousy to consume us and thus corrupt our response to the visitation of the Holy One. **3**. It really helps us to deal with this if we understand that *God is not always fair, but is always just.* I can find no scriptural basis for fairness by God. If you think everyone should have the same amount of money, live in the same kind of house, and possess the same level of intelligence, you are misunderstanding the fact that it is His vineyard. Yes, some of that is predicated upon our efforts and application. But, let's face it. He blesses some in ways He doesn't others. He is the king. The sooner we resign ourselves to that fact and cease grumbling about our pay, the sooner we will learn to be productive, contributing constituents in this great, ultimate kingdom.

Is it possible that you have been viewing yourself as a Christian, but not as a subject in a kingdom? Have you given real thought to how to relate to a king? **The** King? I hope the word government does not bother you, because that is the best way to describe the kingdom. May He give us the grace to be good subjects in this overcoming kingdom. *"For He delivered us from the domain of darkness, and transferred us to the kingdom of His beloved Son."* Colossians 1:13

The kingdom of God is like . . .

THE KING!!!

Permission or Purpose?

One of the things that concern me about this society in which we live is the seemingly growing attitude of striving for the minimum. It seems that we are only interested in the "daily minimum requirements." Whatever might be the venture we are involved in, we usually ask ourselves, "What is the least I can get away with?" While in former years this nation had a formidable work ethic, (see "Why America Doesn't Work" by Chuck Colson) employees today constantly explore what is the least they can do and still get by, while at the same time seeking the highest wage possible. If you are ever around a job site of any kind you will surely hear someone bragging about how many hours they "didn't do a thing" and yet were paid for that time. Even in our purchasing of products, there is a segment of our society that simply wants ". . . the cheapest thing I can find." While no one wants to spend money foolishly or unnecessarily extravagant, nevertheless, this striving for the minimum has caused us to forget things like quality, wise investment of our money, and how soon we want to replace a product. Excellence is a virtue I would, personally, like to see return to every facet of our living together on this great planet. Not surprisingly, the church is not exempt from this mentality of striving for the minimum. When less than 5% of "Christians" in America obey God with a tenth of their income that tells me a large portion of the church has been seeking the minimum. And while this is another subject for maybe another newsletter, allow me to point out that the tithe *is* the minimum and not the ultimate. Nevertheless, the fact is that an inability by 95% of the church to fulfill a basic directive set forth in the Scriptures reveals to me a deeper problem. That is a spirit of religion which has infiltrated the church, causing people to determine the least they can get away with, rather than seeking the ultimate purpose of God and endeavoring to walk therein. I would rather have to deal with a demon-possessed person than with a religious spirit. I personally consider the religious spirit more vile. Religion always causes one to seek the lowest point of responsibility.

Seeking the lowest level of demand is the exact opposite of our Father's extension of Himself to us. He has never sought to give us the least He can get away with and has never asked us to settle for second best. The creation of the earth, mankind, and all the animals was anything but striving for the minimum. And when it was time to send an emissary to earth to redeem us, He sent the very best He had, His only son. *Anything less than excellence falls short of being accurate representatives of God in the earth.*

This is not a new issue that just appeared in the 20th century, but has always been present whenever religion has replaced a true relationship with our Lord. Jesus had to deal with this spirit and we see one instance recorded in Matthew's account, chapter 19, and verses 1-10. Jesus told the Pharisees that although Moses gave them **permission** to divorce their wives, it was because of their stubborn hearts and was not the ultimate **purpose**. When we allow our hearts to become hardened to the Word of God, we begin to seek permission. Note that the Pharisees weren't the only ones trying to determine what they could get away with. I can hear Peter saying to John, "I sure am glad that old Pharisee asked that question. Let's see what he answers." At the end of the passage, it was the disciples who replied if that is the way they should relate to their wives, they would be better off unmarried. Were they seeking the ultimate purpose of God or permission to do what was in their hearts?

What is permission? It is the seeking to lay down the ultimate purpose of God for our lives and doing the minimum. It gives us some feeling of satisfaction because we are doing something good;

sometimes even for God. Even though large crowds followed the Son of God and he healed them, the Pharisees were still only interested in finding a spiritual loophole. When you go from living by relationship with the Most High God to being religious, you have moved back into the arena of laws, rules, and regulations. This is why the Pharisees were trying to determine the minimum the law allowed. What the Pharisees, and most Christians, failed to understand was that the law was not God's ultimate intention. The law was given for violators. It was intended to raise a standard by which we could judge ourselves according to the nature of our Creator. Also, it was set forth to create in us an awareness that we do not have the ability to live by the letter of the law and therefore cause us to seek a higher source of life, strength, and ability. That ability comes from a personal, first-hand relationship with the one who made us in the first place. The Son is the highest revelation of the Father to us. (see Hebrews 1:3) The law, on the other hand, is the minimal revelation of God. When we try to meet the minimum, we have missed the purpose of our God. But when we walk in His purpose, we walk in grace. Are you a person who seeks God's permission to do the minimum and find a loophole or do you embrace His purpose for you and fit yourself into it?

I would like to make four observations concerning the Lord's purpose. One definition of a teacher that I use is an "identifier." I can't teach you to embrace the purpose of God, but I can help identify what it looks like so you can choose to embrace it. And if we are going to seek the Lord's purpose, it will help to understand a little about the impact and dynamic it possesses.

First of all, we must understand that **the Lord's purposes prevail over man's plans.** Proverbs 19:21 says, "*Many are the plans in a man's heart, but it is the Lord's purpose that prevails.*" Also, in Proverbs 16:9, "*In his heart a man plans his course, but the Lord determines his steps.*" Now, there is nothing wrong with planning and setting a course as best we can according to the revelation we now have. As a matter of fact, it is quite necessary for us to be successful in our endeavors. Remember, if we aim at nothing, we will surely hit it. But, we must realize we don't have all the revelation we *will* have and we must be open to the Most High changing our plans by revealing more. Thus, His purpose must prevail over our plans.

Secondly, it is important for us to know that **His purposes will prevail over the plans of nations.** Let's read Psalms 33:10-12. "*The Lord foils the plans of the nations; He thwarts the purposes of the peoples. But the plans of the Lord stand firm forever, the purposes of His heart through* *all generations.*" I recommend you go to your Bible and read the 33rd Psalm to see a larger picture. What we learn from verses 10-12 is that even though it may not appear so at any given time, no nation of people will stop the purpose of God from being carried out and fulfilled. I am aware that as we look at our own nation, supposedly a godly nation, we don't see much room for the plans and purposes of our Lord. But we can rest assured God will foil the plans of even this nation and move it out of the way, before He will allow His own purpose to crumble.

The third observation is that **our Father does not fulfill His purpose by some metaphysical means, but rather uses mankind.** Isaiah prophesied in chapter 46, verses 10b-11, "*My purpose will stand, and I will do all that I please. From the east I summon a bird of prey from a far-off land, **a man to fulfill my purpose.** What I have said, what will I bring about; what I have planned, that will I do.*" The Lord and His purposes always show up in mankind. He intentionally designed it so that His highest form of earthly creation would be His vessel to speak into the earth and represent Him. If we understand that, then we will approach one another, and all people, with a renewed awareness of the fear of God. The saddest thing that can happen is for the Lord to have to pass us by and not use us because we have begun to seek the minimum rather than the purpose in our lives.

The last observation is simply this; **with or without you and me, God's purpose will stand and nothing or no one can frustrate Him**. Again in Isaiah 14:27, *"For the Lord Almighty has purposed, and who can thwart (frustrate) Him?"* His plan is established and purposed and there is no one who can frustrate His plans. I will point out there is one exception to this principle. Because God will not force His will on us, we do have the ability to thwart what He determines in our *own personal lives*. We can literally tie His hands if we ultimately refuse to obey His word to us. His overall purpose will stand, for as He said in one place, if necessary He can have the rocks and trees cry out His purpose in the earth. With a force that mighty and unstoppable, doesn't it make sense for us to get aboard that wave and ride it out all the way to the end? Yes Lord, we will ride!

It will help us to examine the reaction of some of the people to the purpose of God, as recorded in the Scriptures. Also, note the things (or people) they weighed against the purpose of the Lord and see if you have struggled with similar dilemmas.

In the 11th chapter of Hebrews we have an accounting of several of the saints and their life experiences. In verse 7 we see that **Noah saw the** *purpose of God higher than personal humiliation and embarrassment.* He endured 120 years of jeering, mocking, and snide remarks from the people of his community. And I imagine his own family had some questions they would like answered. I can hear son Shem (no, he wasn't on the Three Stooges) now, "So, dad, let me get this straight. The reason we are building this oversized boat on dry land is that water that has been coming up out of the ground is now going to somehow fall from the sky and flood the whole earth?" Of course, we know that once it began to rain, there was no ridiculing or jumping overboard. Through all of this Noah maintained a holy fear toward the purpose of God in his life.

In verses 8-10, we recall Abraham signed a blank check. *"Leave your country . . . and go to the land **I will** show you."* He **embraced the purpose of God as higher than his place of comfort with his natural family and in the land where he grew up**. There is nothing wrong with wanting to be with your natural family or being in the place where you grew up; unless it gets in the way of the purpose of God for you. So Abraham signed the blank check, and then set out on a journey knowing the Most High would fill in the blanks as they went along.

In verses 17-19, we find that ***Abraham saw the purpose of God higher than holding on to the only vehicle for fulfillment of the promise, Isaac.***

You and I would probably have said, "I rebuke you devil! I have received this promise and I will not give it up!" The Father wanted Abraham to learn and wants us to learn to not focus our attention and seeking on the promise, but rather, on the One giving the promise. It is important to note here that the God who told him to sacrifice his son is the same one who also told him to stop and *not* sacrifice Isaac. If we are guilty of holding on to something He told us to do before, to the exclusion of daily communion with Him, we might miss Him trying to change our direction and possibly even sacrifice our blessing on the altar of dullness of hearing.

In verse 23, we see that **Moses' parents saw the purpose of the Most High to be supreme to the king's command**, and thus hid him for three months before devising a brilliant scheme to have him cared for by his own mother in Pharaoh's palace. And then, in verses 24-26 having discovered his true identity, Moses chose the purpose and destiny of God higher than the riches and treasure he might have had as the son of Pharaoh's daughter. He even chose to be mistreated as a son of God because he was looking for a higher reward.

Finally, in verses 32-38, we find some named and some unnamed people who **considered the purpose of God higher than escaping persecution** and, in some cases, even death. And, we think we have trouble when the biggest obstacle some of us have is getting out of bed and going to church on Sunday morning.

In closing, let's read Hebrews 11:39-12:3. *"These were all commended for their faith, yet none of them received what had been promised. God had planned something better for us so that only together with us would they be made perfect. Therefore, since we are surrounded by such a great cloud of witnesses, let us throw off everything that hinders and the sin that so easily entangles, and let us run with perseverance the race marked out for us. Let us fix our eyes on Jesus, the author and perfecter of our faith, who for the joy set before Him endured the cross, scorning the shame, and sat down at the right hand of the throne of God. Consider Him who endured such opposition from sinful men, so that you will not grow weary and lose heart."* We can join with the great cloud of witnesses that surrounds us; those witnesses who paid the price long ago to walk in the ultimate purpose of God and thus blaze the trail ahead of us so we could do the same. I also believe they are cheering us on, so their efforts will not have been in vain. Because of those witnesses and the Great Witness, let us lay aside, by an act of our will, the thing or things that prevent us from walking in the ultimate purpose of God for our lives. Let us fix our gaze on the Son who endured the cross for the joy set before Him to please His Father. If we remind ourselves He was a real person with real feelings and emotions that endured a tremendous amount of hostility to fulfill His purpose in God, then we will not grow weary and lose our sense of purpose and determination.

PERMISSION OR PURPOSE?
CHOOSE PURPOSE!!

The Prodigal Who Strayed

About two months ago I wrote down my topics for the first six issues of the Kernels of Truth for this year, and what I wrote for this month is the topic of the prodigal son. On two separate Sundays following, the local pastor spoke about the prodigal. Since then, I have heard two radio ministers speaking on the same subject. How dare they read my notes! (Just kidding.) But seriously, in this little story contained in the 15th chapter of Luke, we find a wealth of information that can help us as we pursue this life with our Lord. Probably no one reading this letter is in danger of totally walking away from his or her life with God. That's not what this newsletter is about. It is about the little things that prevent us from experiencing the totality of what God desires for us. By observing this story, maybe we can avoid being infected with the spirit of the prodigal in those little things that so easily beset us.

A little over 23 years ago, I was present at a conference in Leesburg, Florida when the late Don Basham spoke on the two prodigals; the Prodigal Who Strayed and the Prodigal Who Stayed. While I remember very little of his content from that meeting, and do not have the notes, I couldn't arrive at a better title, so I am borrowing them for this newsletter and the next one also. I will not provide the main text in this letter, so it would be good if you could read Luke 15:11-32.

Jesus is attracting the tax collectors and "sinners" of the day as He expounds the gospel to those around Him. You know, that hasn't changed. If we will deliver the unadulterated, non-religious message, we will attract those who need it most, even today. The religious society of the day, represented aptly by the Pharisees and teachers of the law, were aghast at the very thought that this *"man welcomes sinners and eats with them."* Then Jesus began to use stories to demonstrate to His listening audience the value God places on one of His wayward children. In the parable of the lost sheep, and then the parable of the lost coin, He makes it clear that God and the angels rejoice greatly when one of these sinners repents and comes home. Then he delves into this story, one about a man who had two sons. As we will see later, this one was particularly aimed at the Pharisees.

We find this younger son, for whatever reason, asks for his part of his father's inheritance. With some delay, he strikes out on his own for a distant country. I must admit there is a certain characteristic about this man that I admire. He was willing to take a risk. He wasn't satisfied with the status quo, and was willing to "roll the dice" to find a better way. We know that his choices were flawed, but we all need a good dose of being willing to step out of the norm to pursue a dream.

The story doesn't identify for us much of the timetable, but at some point the young man had squandered his whole inheritance on loose living. There developed a famine in the land, and this young man found himself working for a pig farmer. When he realized the pigs were eating better than he was, he came to his senses. I suppose that would do it. A spirit of repentance came upon him, and he set out for his homeward journey. By this time, he was willing just to be a servant in his father's house, if it meant he could cease living with the pigs and get a decent meal. A rather lively party ensued when the father received his son back home. The older son wasn't willing to participate, but we will deal with him next month. There are several lessons we can pick up from this story, and I would like to deal with them here.

First of all, the wayward son **thought that he knew better than his father what he needed**. We father's have this uncanny knack of dumbing-down whenever our children reach their early to mid-teens. I don't know exactly how this dynamic works so consistently each time, but our progressive level of ignorance seems to be directly related to the increasing age of our teenage offspring. And then an even more amazing thing occurs. When these same children reach an age of 22-25, our intelligence miraculously returns! Pity the father that doesn't have any teenagers to help him through this process. It appears this phenomenon was happening in this story. This young man obviously thought he knew a whole lot more about what he needed than did his father, despite his years of experience and wisdom. Before we pronounce judgment on this fellow, is it possible that we sometimes question that God knows what we need better than we? We would never speak such, but I think our actions often demonstrate this attitude. To avoid even a small dose of prodigalism, (my spell checker just short-circuited on that one) we need to really believe that "Father Knows Best" and always has our best interests at heart, even when we don't understand. (See Jeremiah 29:11)

Another thing that I think contributed to his desire to leave was **he didn't want to be like his older brother**. The exposure of elder brother's heart and attitude in the end of the story wouldn't have been the only time these characteristics showed up in him. Could you and I be guilty of sometimes looking at a brother or sister and allowing their shortcomings to foster an attitude that says "I will give up and make a fast exit?" It is not a good thing when we let someone else dictate our frame of mind, but we should allow others the room to err while we walk with God on our own. One character trait I see diminishing in this age is one of responsibility for our own actions. It doesn't matter how many people around us may fail, we are ultimately going to answer to the Father for our own actions and blaming someone else will not suffice.

An all too common error this young man made was *he didn't have a thankful attitude. He didn't identify and count his blessings*. It is obvious he had forgotten the seeming comfort that surrounded him, and he definitely, if only temporarily, forgot that he had a father who loved him tremendously. He certainly focused more on what he didn't have than that which he did have. in Acts chapter 3, when Peter and John approached the temple to pray, they were stopped by a crippled man begging for alms. (He asked for alms and got legs; sorry, I couldn't resist.) Peter replied he had no money, but the man was welcome to what he did have. We must be able to focus on what we have been blessed with instead of moaning about what we have not yet received. An attitude of gratitude will guard us at all times against attempting to hurry up the blessing process. Let us count our blessings; yes, let us name them one by one. Do you want to maintain a right attitude at all times and allow God to complete his work in you? Always be grateful. A grateful heart would have prevented this man from going away to his near demise.

One thing that is most obvious is **he was infected with "the grass is always greener on the other side" syndrome.** This principle is as sure as the law of gravity. It is always with us. Sitting on the front porch of that apparently large farmhouse, this fellow looked down the road, past the mailbox, and dreamed about another, more romantic land and developed a desire that overwhelmed his reason. It always looks better on the other side of the fence, because we don't have all the facts concerning life on that side. One thing we must remember, there can be a thin line between the "grass is always greener on the other side" syndrome and a legitimate desire to allow God to take us to a place we have never known. I believe there should be a little explorer in each of us, which will keep us from finding a resting-place along our journey. There are many safeguards in place that can help protect us against making a mistake in judgment, such as leadership, fellowship with our brothers and sisters, and adhering to sound teaching. Accountability will help us handle responsibility and not run down the road after the wrong dream.

Here is another lesson we can learn from this story. ***The noblest of causes that are fueled by human effort usually wind up in the pigpen.*** In an age of political correctness, we can be fooled into believing the nobility of the cause is reason enough for our being involved. But, what should always be the guiding reason for our involvement is the word of God; the voice of God directing our paths. David records in Psalm 29 that *"the voice of the Lord is powerful; the voice of the Lord is majestic . . . The voice of the Lord makes the deer give birth."* Let us rely on hearing from our God and not be swayed simply by a need or desire. It will help you stay out of your own private pigsty.

The father in this story demonstrates a characteristic of God that we need to understand. ***God will allow us to come to the end of ourselves in the pigpen.*** Sometimes, the best thing that the Father can do is to step back and allow us to reach the end of our rope so we will then reach for His rope, which is our salvation. The way back starts when we do come to the end of our own devices. The father in Luke 15 didn't go off into the foreign land looking for his son so he could berate him into returning. He patiently waited, probably sometimes better than others, for the day the wayward soul would return into his fold. If we are stubborn enough to seek our own way, our God will give us the liberty to explore that which we so desire. This is judgment. We think of judgment as God pounding us on the head and condemning our actions, but it is simply the Father giving us over to our desires that we have insisted upon. The judgment of God is a demonstration of His mercy to us. Then when we have reached the end of our way, He is always waiting with open arms for our return, ready to kill the fattened calf and bring forth the royal robes and signet ring.

One thing that I must add to this subject is that **we should beware the gospel that gives robes in the pigsty**. The son received the robe upon returning home. The father wasn't looking for perfection in his son before he brought out the robe and ring, which I believe, by the way, signifies royalty. He was simply looking for him to return. We do an injustice to a soul when we convey to them that somehow they could achieve, even while in the pigpen, enough good works that they deserve to be robed with the royalty of God. This is a great disservice because none of us can do enough to deserve the awesome grace of God He wishes to bestow upon us. It is upon our moving from the pigsty towards the Father. This is repentance. All God wants from us is just a little movement. Direction is everything in your walk with God. Change the direction in which you are facing and you will be deluged with the robe of righteousness.

The ultimate lesson in this story is the **importance the Father places on our returning** into the fold once we are one of those wayward ones. And the rejoicing that takes place in heaven upon the return of a prodigal son or daughter should spill over into the earth for us to join with the angels. Nothing delights our God more than for one of His created ones to give up the fight and yield to His drawing on their soul.

Maybe you aren't a wayward soul, but you know of one. God is emphasizing in this hour the effectiveness of one to one evangelism. Allow Him to use you in a relationship with a stray one to see them leave their foreign land and return to the one who created them for a higher purpose. Pray for Him to cause you to have divine appointments with lost people and to help you develop divine relationships with them also. Then you can help the heavenly host go get the robes and signet rings as the Father says, "Let's have a party! One who was dead is now alive! One who was lost is now found!"

The Prodigal Who Stayed

"**M**eanwhile, the older brother was in the field." Luke 15:25. I have heard this story most of my life, and possibly so have you. I don't remember too many times hearing about the older son, only the sad state of the younger, rebellious boy. As I have grown older and have had the occasion to deal with people in up close circumstances, I have observed how the older son in this parable was just as much a prodigal as the younger. I like to tell the story about the child who wouldn't sit down in church until his father duly warned (that's translated "threatened") him. Upon sitting down, the child notified the father, "I may be sitting down on the outside, but on the inside, I am still standing up." Well, just because we may be demonstrating the correct behavior, it doesn't necessarily mean that our inner attitude is what it should be. The worst case is when we deceive even ourselves into thinking that the outward actions are enough if we are abiding by the rules. I think that is exactly where the older sibling in Jesus' parable found himself. The return of the younger brother was not only a time of rejoicing because "he who was dead is alive again," it was a time of confrontation for the other brother to be able to deal with his inner frustrations and deceptions. Last month we dealt with the younger brother and this month I want to look at this older son and glean what we can from his experience with this episode.

By inference of the title, one doesn't have to leave to be a prodigal. It may be possible that the prodigal who does and says all the right things is actually in more danger than the one who blatantly rebels. The younger son had no trouble recognizing his sin and promptly repenting; returning immediately to his father. But, big brother had a little more difficulty figuring out he had a problem, simply because he was still there. Don't think for a minute that I condone willful sin; I am simply attempting to expose the deception of religion in our lives. And that's exactly what Jesus was attempting to reveal. The older son, in this parable, is largely representative of the Pharisees and teachers of the day. They were the religious crowd who thought they had it all together and looked down their noses at everyone else. Now let's look at some observations concerning the *prodigal who stayed*.

The first thing I see with this young man is that **he was infected with "Marthaism."** Maybe Jesus still had Martha on his mind when he told this parable, as that event occurred not too long before his delivery of this story. In Luke 10:38-42 we read how that Martha was busy to the point of distraction with all kinds of things she felt necessary to do, while her sister sat at the Lord's feet listening to what He had to say. Martha couldn't slow down long enough to know how to rest in the presence of the Messiah, but she was consumed with all the activity. How easy it is to mistake *religious activity* for a *proper relationship* with the Lord. This was especially rampant in the early days of the charismatic renewal. People were finding a new power and perspective in their walk with the Lord, and often allowed themselves to slowly ease into a frame of mind that says, "The more I do and the more meetings I can attend, the more spiritual I am." I remember a story Brother Charles Simpson told in the early 1970's about a reporter interviewing people in a retirement center. This reporter was gathering information from the senior citizens about the secrets to their longevity. The first gentleman he came to replied to the question, "I have never touched a drop of alcohol, never had any tobacco in my body, and I always got plenty of exercise and rest." Interesting thought the reporter. "How old are you, sir?" "Eighty-seven years old." Next, he came to a lady and her reply was like this. "I think it is tied to proper diet as well as keeping a clear conscience at all times." The reporter wrote that reply down and then asked her age. "I am proud to say I am ninety-two years old." He then came to an elderly looking white-haired gentleman and asked him his secret to longevity. "Well, first you must understand, I am a charismatic. I spent most of my time going to prayer meetings, Bible studies and praise-fests. I attended something every night of the week, and sometimes during the day. I anxiously ran to every conference or seminar that was within a reasonable distance. I also actually found time to attend church twice on Sunday." "Wow!" extolled the reporter. "How old are you, sir?" "Oh, I'm 35 years old." Activity may not put you and I in the nursing home, but it will certainly distract us from what is really important, a communicating relationship with our Savior. Guard yourself against "Marthaism."

Maybe the biggest problem the older son faced was that **he didn't understand what was already his or who he was**. His father told him, upon learning of his concern, ". . . *you are always with me and everything I have is yours.*" He had all the family estate, the farm, and his father's wealth at his disposal. It all belonged to him, yet he still felt that somehow it was beyond his grasp. He was probably paranoid of not ever gaining what already belonged to him. How often do we as Christians chase after, and attempt to grasp that which the Father has already promised? Or, how many times do we miss receiving all He has in store for us because we do not have a real sense of who we are in God? Paul wrote to the church in Rome, *"The Spirit himself testifies with our spirit that we are God's children. Now if we are children, then we are heirs---heirs of God and co-heirs with Christ, if indeed we share in his sufferings in order that we may also share in his glory."* Romans 8:16-17. It is important that we understand who we are in God to really understand what we have available to us. Maybe I will do a later newsletter on "Avoiding an Identity Crisis," but for now let me say that our identity should come from what God says about us and not what we do. Neither should our identity come from what others say we are or will be. Know this; the Father makes all that He has and is available to you and me to make us complete citizens in the kingdom of God. We don't need to fear not inheriting our part, nor should we worry that He may have given our part of the package to someone else. You are a unique individual in God's eyes with unique requirements and a very unique destiny. Do you sometimes look at how God has blessed another brother or sister and wonder how He could so abundantly give to them when you have been so loyal and committed? The older brother had the same question. What he failed to understand, and what we need to realize, is that what the father in this story gave to the younger son was already his to begin with. It was his inheritance. Instead of looking at someone else's blessing with disdain, let us say "Hallelujah, there's more where that came from, and I have an inheritance waiting on me."

I also think that the eldest son was **presumptively judgmental**. We recall his response to his father - "*But when this son of yours who has squandered your property with prostitutes comes home, you kill the fattened calf for him!*" If the younger brother had just returned home, and the elder brother was just learning of his arrival, how could he have known that his brother or "this son of yours" was entertaining prostitutes? He not only was judgmental towards his brother, but he was presuming some things for which he had nothing to base them upon. What would cause him to simply assume something so vile without even speaking to the younger son? I think the next character flaw in this boy helps us, maybe, to understand.

Part of him wished that he had the nerve to go away like his brother. "Me thinks he protesteth too much." That line from Shakespeare tells a large part of the story. Why would he assume that his brother had squandered his fortune on "ladies of the evening?" I believe it is because *that is what was in his own heart*. One thing I learned years ago when counseling people is that most of the time, when someone is given to exaggerated railing about a particular sin, that is usually the area in which they themselves struggle. As you may recall, one of the things I admired about the younger son was his willingness to take a risk. The older son probably disliked himself because he did not have the courage to take a risk. I believe there was a certain amount of jealousy because while he watched his younger sibling chase a dream, he knew that he could never step out of his comfort zone. Now, understand I am not by any stroke of the imagination excusing running off and squandering what God has given us on wild living. I am simply saying I think we all could use a good dose of courage to step out of our safe haven and explore some areas, previously unknown to us, where God wants to take us.

The older son was also deceived into believing in a performance-based righteousness. How easy it is for us to slip into a mentality that says we will become closer to God based on how we are able to perform before Him. Allow me to say here that it is crucially important what we do or don't do in our walk as Christians. But, we can no more improve our righteousness by doing the right things than a dog can improve his chances of being a dog by barking loudly. As a matter of fact, in some neighborhoods, he might just diminish his chances of *remaining* a dog by barking loudly. (That has no spiritual significance; so don't read anything into it.) The word righteousness is defined the simplest by the words "right standing" or "right relationship." Our standing or relationship with God is due to the work of Jesus, not anything we could or would do. II Corinthians 5:21 tells us that *"God made Him who **knew no** sin to **become** sin so that **we might become** the <u>righteousness</u> of God in Christ."* Paul also wrote in Romans 1:16 & 17, *"I am not ashamed of the gospel, because it is the power of God for the salvation of everyone who believes: first the Jew, then for the Gentile. For in the gospel a **righteousness from God** is revealed, a **righteousness that is by faith** from first to last, just as it is written: 'The righteous shall live by faith.'"* Even in the Old Testament we are told in Genesis 15:6 that Abraham believed God and it was credited to him as righteousness. Our performance keeps us healthy in our walk and maintains the lines of communication between the Father and us. But nothing we do or say can change the fact that we have a righteousness that comes from God fully imputed by his love. The older son thought that the more he worked in the field and did all the right things, the more likely he was to inherit all that his father had. There is nothing wrong with working hard and trying to do the right things. The problem comes in the next area of concern with this young man.

He never really knew his father's heart. He was no closer than his brother to fully knowing his father's desire and wishes concerning him. The Pharisees were very intent on doing all the right things by the letter of the law, but they never really knew that the heart of God had nothing to do with rules and regulations, but rather with relationship. It is imperative that we find out what the heart of the Father is toward us and for us. We can get a really good idea by studying the Scriptures, but ultimately, there will be no substitute for daily communion by the Spirit with the Sustainer of your soul. The reason the elder brother was surprised when his father threw a welcome home party for his wild younger brother was he never really got to know his father or how he thought. God says His thoughts are higher than our thoughts and His ways are higher than our ways. The only way we can truly get a glimpse of His thoughts is to fellowship with Him having a listening ear. We need to be more concerned with knowing His heart than knowing all the rules and regulations.

The last thing I want to observe about this brother was **he was unwilling to forgive his brother's trespasses**. Unforgiveness will cause you and I great harm and it will affect how we fellowship with the Father. I also may do a letter on Forgiveness because it is probably one of the most important facets of the Christian walk. His refusing to go inside was a telling sign that he wanted nothing to do with this celebration, because he wasn't willing to accept the fact that someone could be freely forgiven for their sin. The reason he thought this way was because he didn't think he could get forgiveness, thus he developed the misconception that he could work his way into this father's good graces. We should be given to rejoicing with God and His angels at the forgiveness of one's sins instead of bemoaning the fact that God should have been harder on them. Jesus put so much importance on this subject that after teaching the disciples the Lord's Prayer, the only part He commented on was when He said, *"For if you forgive men when they sin against you, your heavenly Father will also forgive you. But if you do not forgive men their sins, your Father will not forgive your sins."* Sometimes what people need the most from us is to simply release them from the debt of a wrongdoing and do not count it against them.

Now let me ask you a question. After observing these two sons, which one do you think is more lost? Religion is a defiler of our walk with God, and Jesus was sending a direct message to those Pharisees who had a problem with Him associating with the sinners and tax collectors. He was declaring that while these sinners were able to obtain their forgiveness, these Pharisees could only despise them for not following the same strict regimen of rules they had followed. In Matthew's account of the gospel, Jesus compared them to children who sit in the marketplace and call out to others saying, "We played the flute for you, and you did not dance; we sang a dirge, and you did not mourn." In other words, you are not playing the game the way we think it ought to be played. Therefore, you must be wrong.

May we always have the attitude of the younger son, once he came to his senses, and always come to the Father as His servant. May we never become beset with the problems of the older brother. It is your choice. It is my choice.

Embracing the Future
And Letting Go of the Past

J esus answered, "*Anyone who starts plowing and keeps looking back isn't worth a thing to God's kingdom.*" Luke 9:62 Contemporary English Version. This is the time of year when young people (and some older) are thinking about graduating from high school or college. Having attended a high school graduation myself recently, this was brought home as I watched a group of students pondering in ceremony their destiny and future. This is a hallmark time in each of these lives, a time they can look back on for the rest of their days and remember when they began a new dimension of their journey. Because God is a seasonal or dispensational God, throughout our own journey we can recall many occasions when it seemed He was saying to us, "**From this point forward.**" I realize that some people's idea of a relationship with God involves getting saved, and sitting down somewhere quiet waiting either for the rapture or death so we can go to heaven. The Scripture and my own experience teach me something very different. God is always taking us in a direction. He is always directing our paths by His word and that direction is always forward.

You may find yourself in a place that you know you are entering a new season. A time when you know that the Father is bringing to a close the period of your current life and is preparing you for the next phase of your walk with Him. Please don't ever fall for the lie that He is through with you and can't or won't change you anymore. Our changing walk with Him continues until our death or the Lord Jesus returns. This time of change can be one of the most crucial times of your life, and yet it can be one of the most delightful and fulfilling. How we handle the future as well as our past determines a lot of how we are able to enjoy our time now.

We always have two choices when following God. We can either make **progress**, (going forward), or we can **regress** (going backward). If we are to progress in the kingdom, we will have a mentality of advance and increase. We must look eagerly to what He desires to bring us into next, all the while avoiding disdain for where we have been. I know there have many times in my life when I look back and have been amazed at my own blindness and wonder how I could have been so mistaken about things. How could I have been so shallow? And the Holy Spirit reveals to me that for that particular season, God had me in the shallow end of the pool for a reason. Hindsight truly is the best foresight. We must be able to embrace where He is taking us even though we may not be able to see the full destination. Listen to these words from the book of Hebrews describing some people who understood the idea of embracing the future with eagerness. *"All these people were still living by faith when they died. They did not receive the things promised; they only saw them and welcomed them from a distance. And they admitted that they were aliens and strangers on earth. People who say such things show that they are looking for a country of their own. If they had been thinking of the country they had left, they would have had opportunity to return. Instead, they were longing for a better country, that is, a heavenly one. Therefore God is not ashamed to be called their God, for He has prepared a city for them. These were all commended for their faith, yet none of them received what had been promised. God had planned something better for us so that only together with us would they be made perfect."* Hebrews 11. Now those people not only went after what God had for them with enthusiasm, they also didn't spend a lot of time trying to return to where they had come from. That is regression; returning to an earlier state or going back.

Regression is the thing we most want to avoid. It is the one thing that will prevent us from seizing the future God has prepared for us. To obtain our future we must let go of the past and violently grasp whatever is forward. One of the problems with regression is that it romanticizes the past and contradicts God's promise for the future. On more than one occasion the children of Israel told Moses and Aaron, *"Is it not enough that you have brought us up out of a land flowing with milk and honey to have us die in the wilderness, . . ."* Or, *"We remember the fish which we used to eat free in Egypt, the cucumbers and the melons and the leeks and the onions and the garlic, but now our appetite is gone. There is nothing at all to look at except this manna."* Somehow when times get tough, the past always looks romantic to us. These people had forgotten five hundred years of slave labor. They had forgotten making bricks without the benefit of straw. Even sadder, they had forgotten their joy when God delivered them from the clutches of Pharaoh at the hand of Moses. Learn a lesson from them. If you maintain a posture of progression, going forward, you will not be subject to this type of thinking.

Trying to relive or romanticize the past has been the demise of a great number of believers. I would like to help us avoid this trap if at all possible. How should we deal with the past? How can we properly handle what is behind us? Allow me to attempt to shed some light on this subject.

First of all, we should ***allow the past to help us identify our heritage in God***. Your heritage in

God is very important in helping you develop your own identity in Him. We should regard Hebrews 11 as part of our heritage, viewing our forefathers listed in this chapter as those who went before us to blaze a trail that we wouldn't have to blaze one day. Anyone who reads many of these newsletters or is around me very much, knows how much value I place on my spiritual heritage from having been involved with Brother Charles Simpson and Brother Curtis Forman. I wouldn't change any of that. I also wouldn't want to go back and relive any of my past, as good as most of it was. That would be regression. But, I can have fond memories of times that enriched my soul and helped me get through some very difficult times. Teach your children their heritage both spiritually and naturally, as it is vitally important to them developing who they are in God.

Another value of the past is **it can be a reminder to us of the faithfulness of God**. Sometimes the only thing that will get you and me through a particular situation is remembering a time when God came through and saved us from imminent destruction (or hunger). When faced with the land of the giants, instead of reducing our chances to that of a grasshopper, we should remember the wall of fire and the parting of *our* Red Sea to allow deliverance from our own Pharaoh. It will help us to trust God in our present circumstance if we have a healthy recollection of His intervention sometime in our history.

Someone once said that he who doesn't learn from history (or the past) is destined to repeat it. I would say **the past can be a source of remembering lessons we have learned along the way.** "Burn me once, shame on you. Burn me twice, shame on me." I'm sure you have heard that one. If we will adopt a legitimate view of our history, we will be less likely to repeat the same mistakes that so devastated us before. It's not a bad idea to establish some kind of focal point to be a reminder to us. The nation Israel set up twelve stones at Gilgal as a memorial to the deliverance God had wrought. We can have these same types of memorials for reminding us of our own being set free, or those times when the Father taught us a very valuable lesson.

We should be able to **let go of some things even if they are things that God gave us in the past.** Abraham heard a clear word from God to go up the mountain and sacrifice Isaac. He went up obediently taking his son along with him. He had full intentions of obeying the command of God to him, knowing that Isaac was a gift from God to begin with, and therefore, the Father could replace him if necessary. Upon raising the knife to slay the promise (don't miss that), the angel of the Lord shouted from heaven, "Abraham! Abraham! Don't slay the boy!" Abraham could have very well replied, "I have a word from God to slay this boy, and so, I rebuke you devil for contradicting that word." The angel shouted because he knew that Abraham's plan was to carry out God's word. But Abraham wasn't holding so tightly to what God had spoken in the past that when God changed direction, Abraham couldn't hear and respond accordingly. Do we hold on to what God has legitimately used in our lives but now wants to take us past? Jesus had just resurrected and appeared to Mary Magdalene. When she attempted to lay her hands on Him, He replied, "*Do not hold on to me, for I have not returned to the Father.*" Jesus, whom the Scripture identifies as the embodiment of the Word of God, asked Mary Magdalene to try not to hold him back from the fulfillment of his destiny, which was to go to His Father. Sometimes we want to create a nice little box in which to confine God's Word to us, so it will fit our predetermined agenda. This stems from an inability to embrace the future and a desire to hold on to the past. Mary wanted Him just like she remembered. She didn't want to deal with a new Jesus who had to go to the Father.

Here is something else. ***Clinging to those "good ole days" is evidence we have no confidence in God and His ability to establish something new in our lives***. Maybe it's a place of comfort that we cling to when we long for the good ole days. But, as I pointed out earlier, those "good ole days" are not always as good as we fool ourselves into remembering. We simply like the familiar rather than the unknown because we have little faith in our God to take us somewhere new. It may also be an indicator that we aren't willing to make the sacrifice sometimes necessary to go on to the next arena the Father is attempting to direct us.

Closely related to that, "***Gimme that ole time religion" is nothing more than assuming the position of the ostrich***. If we can bury ourselves in the past, we will be able to avoid what God has next for us, and then escapism wins again. How many believers hide behind some argument that attaches them unhealthily to the past, so they won't have to be bothered with dealing with their future? This may offend some, and I apologize in advance, but when I see a bumper sticker that says "The King James Bible, the only true Bible," I wonder what that person is running from and avoiding. I wonder what it is God has attempted to change in them that motivates them to retreat into the past so vehemently. Of course when they make a statement like, "The King James Bible was good enough for Jesus and Paul and Silas, and it is good enough for me," I wonder some other things.

One of Jesus' most prominent quotes is when He says, "*Remember Lot's wife!*" Lot's wife while being led to deliverance, tried in her heart to keep her old life when she looked back. A part of her still yearned for what she had in Sodom and she couldn't resist turning and longingly gazing upon where she had come from. At that point, she ceased being a person moving forward towards God's ultimate purpose, and became nothing more than a monument. A monument to the condition of one who insists on living in the past and is unable to embrace the future God has designed for them.

Wherever you find yourself, or whatever season you are approaching, embrace what's ahead, allowing the past to have a healthy influence in your life, rather than become a place of refuge because we are overcome with an attitude of regression. For if you keep looking back, Jesus said you wouldn't be worth a thing for God's Kingdom.

I would like to conclude by saying that this newsletter was inspired partly by a series of teachings delivered by Brother Charles Simpson entitled "Forward On All Fronts." I gained his permission to use some of his material and I want to give credit where credit is due.

Happiness
According to Jesus

H**appiness.** Now _there_ is something that most of modern culture is seeking. People sell all sorts of things and purchase an even more diverse array of items, all the while hoping to arrive at some level of happiness. As good Americans we are given to life, liberty, and the pursuit of happiness. Some think that new boat is going to be the source of the much sought after happiness one so desires. Maybe it's that new house. Far too many divorces occur not too many months after a move into a new home, thinking the new abode will be the cure-all for residing problems. Equally sad, is how many times couples have decided to have an offspring, thinking a child would be the thing that brings happiness into their marriage, only to find out they have brought a child into their vain search for happiness. And sometimes the child suffers because of the shortsightedness of its parents. We think our job or vocation will be our fulfillment and source of the elusive happiness. And, of course, the size of our bank account will surely govern the level of our happiness. It doesn't take someone with a degree in psychology to look around and find some miserable, wealthy people. Of course, there is nothing wrong with boats, babies, new houses, jobs, or large bank accounts. Our problem is that we usually seek happiness in "all the wrong places" as Johnny Lee so aptly sang in the 70's. Jesus taught us *how* to be and *who* would be happy. As is usually the case, the Scriptures are a wealth of resource for us to find out how to achieve real, lasting happiness.

Let's look at Matthew 5:1-11. *"Now when he saw the crowds, he went up on a mountainside and sat down. His disciples came to him, and he began to teach them, saying: 'Blessed are the poor in spirit, for theirs is the kingdom of heaven. Blessed are those who mourn, for they will be comforted. Blessed are the meek, for they will inherit the earth. Blessed are those who hunger and thirst for righteousness, for they will be filled. Blessed are the merciful, for they will be shown mercy. Blessed are the pure in heart, for they will see God. Blessed are the peacemakers, for they will be called sons of God. Blessed are those who are persecuted because of righteousness, for theirs is the kingdom of heaven. Blessed are you when people insult you, persecute you and falsely say all kinds of evil against you because of me.'"* This is commonly called the beatitudes; Brother Bob Mumford called them the Constitution and By-Laws of the Kingdom. Someone has proclaimed they should be called the **be-attitudes**. In these beatitudes, Jesus lays out a picture of the inward attitudes it takes for one to experience the happiness He delivers. As we examine these, I hope you get a larger view of what Jesus is calling us to receive in our inmost being.

There is an angle of achieving happiness in verses one and two of this chapter. Although Jesus doesn't directly address this aspect of achieving happiness, I believe he indirectly communicates it here and directly in other places. Here is what I mean. When Jesus saw the multitude, He turned away from them and went up onto the mountainside. We preachers would never leave the crowd in an attempt to shrink the audience to those succinctly identified as the membership, but Jesus did. The Bible says "*his _disciples_ came to him, and he began to teach them.*" Only those who were counted as His disciples came to where He was on the mountainside. Please note that this crowd was not limited to the twelve. In verse 28 of chapter 7 we find that, "*When Jesus had finished saying these things* (the Sermon on the Mount), *the _crowds_ were amazed at his teaching.*" **Sometimes the Father will cause us to have to climb some mountain to demonstrate our commitment to Him and His Son**. When we are willing to climb the mountain, foray through the difficulty, to get to where the

Father is meeting us, we further solidify our resolve as constituents of His kingdom. And that puts us in a frame of mind and spirit to be teachable at His feet. All this produces a happiness in us, which is signified by contentment.

But then, Jesus begins to teach the disciples by saying, "Blessed are the . . ." Another word for "blessed" is the word "happy". And several modern versions actually use that word in this passage instead of blessed. I must insert here that this is not the shallow, transient happiness that we so often identify in the human race; but rather, this happiness is a deep, abiding contentment that comes from living in the geography of the Beatitudes as Jesus spells them out. To His listeners, He addresses some qualities and characteristics that will lead to true happiness; happiness that will last. Let's look at them one by one and see how accurately they draw a picture of your inward attitudes.

Blessed or Happy are the poor in spirit, for theirs is the kingdom of heaven. First let's identify that He is not teaching the disciples concerning financial poverty, but, rather, the recognizing of the poverty of our spirit. I do not hold to the sometimes extreme, "prosperity" teaching that still remains in certain corridors of the church today, but, neither do I embrace the notion that being broke somehow makes us more spiritual. What

Jesus is addressing here is, if we want true happiness, we need to recognize that we are naturally deficient in and of ourselves before God. When we stand in the presence of the Father, we become aware of our own shortcomings and inabilities. It is incumbent upon us to be able to admit that we need Him, and not join the "pull myself up by my own bootstraps" society. Paul said in his second letter to the church in Corinth, *"Therefore I will boast all the more gladly about my weaknesses,* (deficiencies) *so that Christ's power may rest on me."* He went on to say, *"For when I am weak, then I am strong."* When we come to the end of our own abilities and declare ourselves weak before God, He imparts His strength to us and we are able to live in His victory instead of some false manufactured one. This is because the Father said, *"My power is made perfect* (or complete) *in weakness."* When we are able to get out of the way, or get off the throne, we establish ourselves in a place of humility where we can sit on the mountainside and receive supernatural impartation from the Father through the Holy Spirit. And that place of resignation to His strength is a divine place of contentment that brings us true happiness, according to the words of Jesus. So recognizing our total need of the Father and His provision is the beginning of being happy.

Happy are those who mourn, for they will be comforted. I believe there is a legitimate element here of what we would typically call to mind when we think of mourning. It is correct to say that if something or someone saddens us, the Father desires to comfort us and give us joy instead of mourning. But in the context of what Jesus is teaching here, I would like to look at this mourning with maybe a little different slant. I think that first He sets down the principle that we must accept our ineptness before Him and recognize our poverty of spirit. We must be able to see that it is not the becoming poor in the spirit that leads to happiness, but rather, honestly acknowledging our condition and thus positioning ourselves for the reign of God (the kingdom of heaven is theirs) in our lives. Once we have been forthright with our assessment of ourselves before God, the next natural response, in light of our condition, should be an attitude of mourning. If we truly see our deficiency before God, we will begin to cry out for the grace and mercy of God to fill the void. Jesus told a parable of a Pharisee and a tax collector. The Pharisee prayed about (the NIV margin says he prayed to) himself: *"God I thank you that I am not like all other men— robbers, evildoers, adulterers—or even like this tax collector."* I would say there is no poverty of spirit there. He had, in his opinion, no need. The tax collector, on the other hand, stood at a distance and would not even look up toward heaven. Rather, he began to beat his breast in mourning and prayed, *"God, have mercy on me, a sinner."* The awareness of his spiritual poverty led him to mourn his state of being, and pray for God to have mercy on him. The Lord God summed it up when He declared through the prophet Jeremiah, *"Let not the wise man boast of his wisdom or the strong man boast of his strength or the rich man boast of his riches, but let him who boasts boast about this: that he understands and knows me, that I am the Lord, who exercises kindness, justice and righteousness on earth, for in these I delight."* Jeremiah 9:23-24.

Now let's look at what God promises when we truly admit and accept our poverty of spirit before Him, and cry out to Him to have mercy on us in an attitude of mourning. In Isaiah 61 the prophet delivers a word, about Jesus the Savior that went something like this. *"The Spirit of the Sovereign Lord is on me, because the Lord has anointed me to preach good news to the **poor**. He has sent me to bind up the brokenhearted, to proclaim freedom for the captives, and release for the prisoners, to proclaim the year of the Lord's favor and the day of vengeance of our God, to **comfort** all who **mourn**, and provide for those who grieve in Zion—to bestow on them a crown of beauty instead of ashes, the **oil of gladness** instead of **mourning**, and a garment of praise instead of a spirit of despair. They will be* *called oaks of righteousness, a planting of the Lord for the display of his splendor."* One thing I want to clearly convey is that it isn't walking around with a face a mile long and constantly being in a state of mourning that will produce the happiness of which Jesus speaks. But once we are honest with God and ourselves and make a true assessment of our spirit in His presence, we are faced with the sadness of our lack. He promises that in our mourning, we will be comforted. The happiness comes not from our sadness, but rather from the result of Him giving us "the oil of gladness instead of mourning." It comes not because we have deficiencies in our life, but when, having faced the truth about our deficiencies, we allow Him to be King in our lives.

How do you see yourself before God? If you are not quite as happy as you once remember, maybe a re-posturing would be in order. It is possible for us to get so caught up in activities that we get overly confident in our own abilities and thus cease, at least to some measure, calling out from a mournful heart for God to have mercy on us and impart to us His strength and ability. You see, what happens is that we begin empowered by the grace and mercy of God, and then forget our source, and attempt to continue the journey having forgotten to continually draw from the pool of mercy, grace and strength that got us started in the first place. The more we can rely on Him, call on

Him, fellowship with Him, the happier we will certainly be.

We will continue with the rest of the "be-attitudes" over the next three letters. Until then, may you be overwhelmed with the oil of gladness God will surely visit upon you.

Happiness
According to Jesus (part 2)

L ast month, we began talking about finding true happiness, and allowing the words of Jesus to instruct us as to how to find that happiness. In Matthew 5, Jesus begins His Sermon on the Mount by declaring certain groups of people who would be blessed, or happy. We shared how we first come to God in the poverty of our own ability, and then, we cry out from a heart of mourning for God's grace and mercy to intervene. That brought us through verse 4. Scary, isn't it?

Let's look at the entire passage again and take up in verse 5. Matthew 5:1-11. *"Now when he saw the crowds, he went up on a mountainside and sat down. His disciples came to him, and he began to teach them, saying: 'Blessed are the poor in spirit, for theirs is the kingdom of heaven. Blessed are those who mourn, for they will be comforted. Blessed are the meek, for they will inherit the earth. Blessed are those who hunger and thirst for righteousness, for they will be filled. Blessed are the merciful, for they will be shown mercy. Blessed are the pure in heart, for they will see God. Blessed are the peacemakers, for they will be called sons of God. Blessed are those who are persecuted because of righteousness, for theirs is the kingdom of heaven. Blessed are you when people insult you, persecute you and falsely say all kinds of evil against you because of me.'"*

Blessed are the meek, for they will inherit the earth. Why would Jesus make this statement immediately following a declaration that those who are poor in spirit and mourn will be happy? I am beginning to see this passage as progressive. Jesus knew that after we have eaten from the tree of reality as to our own need for Him, and cried out to God for grace and mercy, that His Father would, because of His nature, begin to impart His strength and grace to us. When Paul said, *"For when I am weak, then I am strong,"* he was demonstrating that he understood the process of accessing true happiness. As we truly place ourselves in a posture to draw from the divine strength pool, we, in fact, **are** strong. When we are weak, we **really do** develop strength, because we are joined to the Great Source of Strength. For you see, it is not God's intention at all for us to go around looking like we are on a perpetual diet of lemon juice. The reason for facing our own deficiencies and lamenting our shortcomings is not to make us depressed, but to bring us up out of the ash heap into a life of vitality and strength unequaled by anything we might find in ourselves. It is God's desire to make someone out of us that can accurately represent the kingdom of God in the earth.

Another thing that God begins to harvest is the ability that is resident in each one of us. We are each gifted with God-given ability to be that which He has designed before the beginning of time for us to be. The Holy Spirit begins to draw out of us that nature of the Most High God that we received at the new birth, and God begins to seek a return on His investment in us. Can you see how that if we will submit to the process of reality, we will begin to become strong, confident, secure individuals who can make an impact on the society in which we live? What does this have to do with the meek inheriting the earth? I have no idea. Just kidding!

Maybe the definition of meekness will help you. The best definition of meekness is **strength under discipline or control**. Without putting words in Jesus' mouth, I believe this is what He was saying. *Once you access the strength of my Father by dealing in the truth about your own abilities, don't be fooled into thinking your newfound strength is yours. Don't allow yourselves to make the mistake of thinking that the anointing of the Holy Spirit has anything to do with you. Submit that newfound strength or ability to my Father, and you will not only inherit the earth, you will be able to rule it with me in the coming age of the kingdom.* God isn't looking for weak people to serve Him in the kingdom, but rather is looking for formerly weak people who have been endued with power from on high, and who have discovered a strength they did not have before. John 1:12 says in the King James Version that *". . . as many as received him, to them he gave power to become the sons of God."* Most modern versions, including the New King James, give a more accurate translation of the word there by saying it this way. *"But as many as received Him, to them He gave the right to become children of God."* The word "power" is translated "authority" or "the right." Now look at Acts 1:8. *"But you will receive power when the Holy Spirit comes on you; and you will be witnesses in Jerusalem, and in all Judea and Samaria, and to the ends of the earth."* The word "power" here is "dunamis." Now if you have been around charismatic or Pentecostal circles you have certainly heard the fact that "dunamis" is where our word "dynamite" comes from. That is accurate. But allow me to tell you that the word "dunamis" is also translated "ability." How does this sound? *When the Holy Spirit comes upon us, we receive ability so effective that it is compared to the impact of dynamite.* If we are going to make an impact on Jerusalem, Judea, Samaria and points beyond, we need to have accessed the flow of strength available to us by drinking from the river of our own reality. But what God doesn't need is for us to forget our source of strength and ability, nor should we forget our poverty of spirit and mourning which brought us to the place of our need. He needs confident, strong individuals who have humbled themselves before the Almighty God. He desires people who quietly absorb their surroundings without destroying everything in sight with their reactions. God doesn't want weak people. He needs meek people. <u>Meekness is strength under discipline</u>.

Blessed are those who hunger and thirst for righteousness, for they shall be satisfied. Recently the leadership of Abundant Life Church declared a 24-hour fast for the future of the congregation. It's amazing how quick, when that is resolved as a definite, one can begin to think about food. I watched teens that obviously have never fasted before, begin to agonize days before the appointed day, knowing they were going a full day without food. It's that kind of hunger that the Father desires from us. We need the kind of hunger and thirst that causes us to dwell on our object of desire. If we are to be truly satisfied, we must acquire an incessant craving for that which completes us in God.

The word righteousness is an often-misunderstood word. Originally the word was spelled "rightwiseness." To better understand "rightwiseness", it will help to look at the term "wise ness." Look at these definitions; _to_ (rightly) _perceive directly: have (_right_) direct cognition of: to_ *have* (right) *understanding of: to* (rightly) *recognize the nature of: to* (rightly) *recognize as being the same as something previously known: to be* (rightly) *acquainted or familiar with: to have* (right) *experience of or with: possessing inside information.* When you put the word "right" or "rightly" in front of each of those definitions, you begin to get a biblical understanding of the righteousness we are admonished to hunger and thirst after. Righteousness is sometimes defined as a "right-standing." There is even a case for the term "right-relationship," especially when we refer to our relationship with the Father. There is an imputed righteousness that we receive from the Father at the new birth, thus we are called the "righteousness of God in Christ." Established forever in heaven is the account that Jesus settled on our behalf, and because He was our substitute on the cross, we obtain His righteousness through no effort or performance of our own. What I think Jesus was addressing here is our necessity for that right standing relationship with the Father of our imputed righteousness. Most of what Jesus and the Scriptures talk about is not dealing with getting us to heaven. It is about helping us to be kingdom citizens while we are still here on the earth. One of the reasons I think that Jesus was not addressing imputed righteousness here is because of the analogy He uses. Hunger and thirst are appetites that return frequently, and call for fresh satisfactions; so these desires rest not in any thing attained, but are carried out toward renewed pardons, and daily fresh supplies of grace. We will never need to hunger for the righteousness that the Father has dressed us with, but we do have a need to walk circumspectly before Him in the light of that righteousness. Jesus uses on many occasions what I call "perpetual terminology." Scholars of the Greek language would call this the "present or continuing tense." In Matthew 7:7, the original language seems to indicate He is saying, "Ask and keep on asking, seek and keep on seeking, knock and keep on knocking." Here is the way that verse reads in the Amplified Bible. *"Keep on asking and it will be given you; keep on seeking and you will find; keep on knocking and the door will be opened to you."* We are leaky creatures. We need to perpetually be seeking. We need to perpetually be hungering and thirsting for that rightness with our God. We need to be filled with the Holy Spirit and keep on being filled. On more than one occasion, the early church was getting filled with the Spirit again. If we are to correctly hunger and thirst for that relationship that allows us to walk out the righteousness He has imputed to us, we must understand it is not a one time affair. It is a lifelong commitment to allow the Father to give healthy appetites for His presence and for His sustenance that comes only through right relationship with Him.

Another point I want to make is concerning the allegories He uses here of hunger and thirst. Hunger is a desire of food that sustains; thirst is the desire of drink that refreshes. Seeking a knowing relationship with our God gives us what we need to sustain us and to provide us the aforementioned strength. Our bodies require food to function. We can go a period of time without the intake of food, but at some point, our body will cease to function if it doesn't receive something to replenish what is missing. If we don't hunger and thirst after righteousness, we will cease being functioning, contributing people of God, and find ourselves on the trash heap of life waiting to go to heaven. How sad would that be? David said, *"I would have despaired unless I had believed that I would see the goodness of the LORD in the land of the living."* In the same fashion, remaining right before the Father will provide us with that which refreshes. We all need those times of rejuvenation and restoration. I think it is part of the conspiracy of the Trinity to place us in such a place that we, out of necessity, must hunger and keep on hungering; thirst and keep on thirsting for a right standing with Him.

God is not necessarily looking for us to be sinless, but He does expect us to be complete. In Matthew 5:48 Jesus says, *"Therefore you are to be perfect, as your heavenly Father is perfect."* The word "perfect" there is from a root word that means to *set out for a definite point or goal.* The word "teleios" means *wanting nothing necessary to completeness.* Again, look at how The Amplified Bible deals with this verse. *"You, therefore, must be perfect* (growing into complete maturity of godliness in mind and character, having reached the proper height of virtue and integrity), *as your heavenly Father is perfect."* He desires to complete us with His presence, but it is going to require a renewable hunger and thirst for Him and for what a communicating relationship with Him delivers.

It is the attitude of meekness that leads us to the place of hungering and thirsting for everything the Father has and is to us.

I am including in this month's letter a paper on meekness from the W.E. Vines Expository Dictionary of New Testament Words, which I find very useful and I hope you will as well. We will continue in the Be-Attitudes next month. Until then, don't worry, be happy. (You knew I couldn't make it through this subject without throwing that one in, didn't you?)

Meekness

Meekness is an inwrought grace of the soul and the exercises of it are first and chiefly towards God. It is that temper of spirit in which we accept His dealings with us as good, and therefore without disputing or resisting; it is closely linked with the word humility. It is only the humble heart which is also the meek, and which, as such, does not fight against God and more or less struggle and contend with Him.

This meekness, however, being first of all a meekness before God, is also such in the face of men, even of evil men, out of a sense that these, with the insults and injuries which they may inflict, are permitted and employed by Him for the chastening and purifying of His elect.

The meaning of the word (for meekness) is not readily expressed in English, for the terms meekness, mildness, commonly used, suggest weakness to a greater or less extent, whereas this word does nothing of the kind. It must be clearly understood, therefore, that the meekness manifested by the Lord and commended to the believer is the fruit of power.

The common assumption is that when a man is meek it is because he cannot help himself; but the Lord was "meek" because he had the infinite resources of God the Father at His command.   Described negatively, meekness is the opposite of self-assertiveness and self-interest; it is calmness of spirit that is neither elated nor cast down, simply because it is not occupied with self at all.

Summed up, <u>meekness is strength under discipline</u>.

Happiness
According to Jesus (part 3)

Blessed are the merciful, for they shall obtain mercy. As we continue our study of the Be-Attitudes, we find ourselves looking at the giving and receiving of mercy. Jesus said that if we want true happiness, one thing we can do is to be merciful towards our fellow neighbor. One of the things I see here again is a progression in our walk of being solid kingdom citizens. We started out being encouraged to recognize our need before the Father and allowing godly sorrow to create in us the desire to rise above our lack. Then we were admonished by Jesus to bring our newfound strength under the discipline of God the Father and greatly thirst for a right relationship with the Lord.

Now after that process, which takes a little longer than the time needed to read these letters, we are instructed by our Lord to begin to display the nature of the Father to those around us. Mercy is a staple of the nature and character of God.

The word "merciful" is translated as "active compassion," or "compassion for the poor." The Lord God always demonstrates His active compassion towards us, His created ones. In Daniel

9:9, 10 and also in I Timothy 1:13, 16 we are told that God shows mercy upon those who have broken His law. Paul also writes to Timothy that he was shown mercy so that in him, the "worst of sinners", Jesus could demonstrate his unlimited patience as an example for those who would believe on him and receive eternal life. Paul writes the church at Ephesus that God is rich in mercy. There is a wealth, or never ending supply of mercy available from our God. In all these examples, we see God actively displaying His compassion on His people. This occurs throughout Scripture both before and after we come to know the Lord. I suppose it is possible that we require more mercy by the Father after we are born again. In either instance, we know that His mercy arrows are always aimed toward us waiting to be fired when needed.

The word "mercy" in the Hebrew is one of the most famous Hebrew words, **chesed**. Pronounced "*cheh-sed*," with almost a hiss, the word appears at least 250 times in the Bible. It is translated loving-kindness, mercy, tenderness, and unfailing love. The closest to communicating the main idea is the word "faithfulness." The Greek counterpart **"*eleos*"** means the outward manifestation of pity; it assumes need on the part of him who receives it, and resources adequate to meet the need on the part of him who shows it. In just about the only bright spot in Jeremiah's

Lamentations, he declares that *"It is because of the Lord's mercy and loving-kindness that we are not consumed, because His tender mercies (or compassions) never fail. They are new every morning . . ."* When he says they are new every morning, he is not exaggerating. Psalm 136 declares twenty-six times that *"His mercy endures forever."* They are new every morning and they endure forever. What hope we have!

In understanding mercy we must be able to differentiate between grace and mercy. Mercy is the aspect of God's nature that causes Him to help the needy, the miserable, the rejected, or the unfortunate. Grace is the aspect of His love that moves Him to forgive the guilty. If we are needy or miserable, it may be so either because we have broken God's law or because of circumstances beyond our control. Remember that mercy is the active compassion by our Lord towards us. The result of that active compassion is that we thusly receive grace that is borne out of that godly compassion. If we look at Titus 3:3-7 it may help even more to see this principle. *"For we also were once thoughtless and senseless, obstinate and disobedient, deluded and misled: (we too were once) slaves to all sorts of cravings and pleasures, wasting our days in malice and jealousy and envy, hateful and hating one another. But when the goodness and loving-kindness of God our Savior to man (as man) appeared, He saved us, not because of any works of righteousness that we had done, but because of His own pity and* **mercy***, by the cleansing of the new birth (regeneration) and renewing of the Holy Spirit, which He poured out so richly upon us through Jesus Christ our Savior. And He did it in order that we might be justified by His* **grace***, (that we might be acknowledged and counted as conformed to the divine will in purpose, thought, and action), and that we might become heirs of eternal life according to our hope."* The Amplified Bible. Because of His *mercy*, we receive *grace*. I Peter 1:3-5 *"Blessed be the God and Father of our Lord Jesus Christ, who according to His great* **mercy** *has caused us to* **be born again** *to a living hope . . ."*

I Peter 2:10 *"For you once were NOT A PEOPLE, but now you are THE PEOPLE OF GOD; you had* **NOT RECEIVED MERCY***, but now you have* **RECEIVED MERCY***."* Because God is merciful, He expects His children to be merciful. Once again, we are commissioned to represent God the Father in the earth by displaying His character and nature. We are called on to demonstrate active compassion to those around us who are needy or dejected. The word compassion means "To come alongside with passion" or to "share their passion." It also means to allow God to cause us to identify with that person's plight. Excuse the quote, but it really is to "feel the other person's pain" and help them in a tangible way to overcome their circumstances. Is it possible that in today's society with its accelerated pace that we have neglected walking with our brother or sister through difficulties because we choose to not have the time? Is it possible that we could, even if temporarily, forget the measure of mercy we received from God ourselves? I think this is the reason Jesus said in Luke 6:36, *"Be merciful, just as your Father is merciful."* A person who is merciful will find outlets for his merciful nature. He will always be cognizant of those around him so he can offer some mercy as Jesus would do if we were present in the flesh. Remember that merciful people are actively compassionate people. It will produce tangible results.

As we are merciful, we will receive mercy. This is both from our fellow man and from God Himself. God has designed His plan so that we can hinder the flow of mercy if we choose to withhold mercy from those with whom we come in contact. Look at the story of the Unmerciful Servant in Matthew 18:23-35 *"For this reason the kingdom of heaven may be compared to a king who wished to settle accounts with his slaves. When he had begun to settle them, one who owed him ten thousand talents was brought to him. But since he did not have the means to repay, his lord commanded him to be sold, along with his wife and children and all that he had, and repayment to be made. So the slave fell to the* ground and prostrated himself before him, saying, 'Have patience with me and I will repay you everything.' And the lord of that slave felt compassion and released him and forgave him the debt. But that slave went out and found one of his fellow slaves who owed him a hundred denarii; and he seized him and began to choke him, saying, 'Pay back what you owe.' So his fellow slave fell to the ground and began to plead with him, saying, 'Have patience with me and I will repay you.' But he was unwilling and went and threw him in prison until he should pay back what was owed. So when his fellow slaves saw what had happened, they were deeply grieved and came and reported to their lord all that had happened. Then summoning him, his lord said to him, "You wicked slave, I forgave you all that debt because you pleaded with me. 'Should you not also have had mercy on your fellow slave, in the same way that **I had mercy on you**?' And his lord, moved with anger, handed him over to the torturers until he should repay all that was owed him. My heavenly Father will also do the same to you, if each of you does not forgive his brother from your heart. Let's be merciful so we can continue to receive our much needed mercy.

Blessed are the pure in heart, for they shall see God. Not in the head; for men may have pure notions and impure hearts; not in the hand, or action, or in outward conversation only, as the

Pharisees were outwardly righteous before men, but inwardly full of impurity; but "in heart". The heart of man is the center of our soul; that which is central to a person. The Hebrew word means, "The seat of one's entire mental and moral activity, containing both rational and emotional elements." It is the seat of feelings, desires, joy, pain, and love. The heart is the dwelling place of the Lord and the Holy Spirit. It is our Grand Central Station. One can easily understand why it would be so important to keep that area of our lives pure. Pure simply means, "Clean; like a vine cleansed by pruning and so fitted to bear fruit; free from every admixture of what is false." It is the keeping our innermost being clear of any activity that would cloud our ability to hear and see God. In the Old Testament, the word "pure" means, "to polish."

It is important for us to keep the vines pruned in our lives, so we do not allow any strange or corrupt thing to grow into our lives. This primarily requires attention to our thoughts. Paul wrote to the Philippians that whatever is true, honorable, right, **pure**, lovely, of good repute, think on these things or to fix your minds on them. Paul also wrote to the Corinthians that we are taking every thought captive to the obedience of Christ. Have you ever heard a computer term, "garbage in; garbage out?" We have this one-pound computer sitting on our shoulders, and the same principle applies. It is important what we give our attention to or fix our minds upon. Our thoughts are the doorway into our hearts, so it behooves us to guard our hearts by guarding our thoughts. Paul precedes his admonishment to the Philippians with this instruction. *Rejoice in the Lord always; again I will say, rejoice! Let your gentle spirit be known to all men. The Lord is near. Be anxious for nothing, but in everything by prayer and supplication with thanksgiving let your requests be made known to God. And the peace of God, which surpasses all comprehension, will* **guard your hearts** *and your minds in Christ Jesus.* Philippians 4:4-7.

To help guard our hearts, it is important that we become lovers of the word of God. The psalmist declares in Psalms 119:9 "*How can a young man keep his way* **pure***? By keeping it according to Your word.*" And again in Psalms 119:140 He says, "*Your word is very* **pure***, therefore Your servant loves it.*" The study of God's word will help keep us pure in heart.

"*Who may ascend the hill of the Lord? Who may stand in his holy place? He who has clean hands and a* **pure heart***, who does not lift up his soul to an idol or swear by what is false.*" Psalm 24:3-4 We all desire to ascend to that holy hill where God resides. And I am not necessarily speaking of heaven, but that place in this life where we can see God with our spirit eyes. The promise is there, in verse 8 of

Matthew 5, that if we are pure in heart, we will experience untold happiness, primarily due to the fact that we will obtain a revelation of God that we did not have before.

Are you looking for happiness? Resolve to become an actively compassionate person from now on, and guard your heart from any interference that will jam the signal from the Most High God. Keep the channels clear so He can speak to you, because He desires to commune with you and me.

When I started this topic, Happiness According to Jesus, I envisioned one, at the most, two newsletters. But as I have gotten into this, I have found there is too much here to condense into one or two.

We will take up with the next Be-Attitudes next month.

Happiness
According to Jesus (part 4)

This month we wrap up our study of the Be-Attitudes, where we find how Jesus describes the path to true happiness. I originally thought this would take one, maybe two newsletters. But as I prepared for this topic, I obviously discovered it required a little more attention than I had anticipated. I thank you for your willingness to follow this topic over the last 3 (and now 4) letters, and also for the many who have personally shared with me how they have been blessed and motivated by these newsletters. And, so, let's move on to the last two *"Blessed's"* in Matthew 5:9-12.

Happy are the peacemakers, for they shall be called the sons (children) of God. What seems to be a simple admonition, may, upon further examination, contain more than we might have ever realized. When we start talking about peacemakers, we must first address the topic of peace.

"Peace" is one of those words that could have a myriad of definitions. Some would think of quiet, some absence of conflict, and even some would define peace as a place of restfulness. None of these are inaccurate. The Hebrew word for peace is "**shalom.**" Here is a list of words that describe the complete meaning of shalom. Completeness, wholeness, peace, health, welfare, safety, soundness, tranquility, prosperity, perfectness, fullness, rest, harmony; the absence of agitation or discord. The root verb of *shalom* means, "to be complete, perfect, and full." Therefore we surmise that *shalom* is the wholeness that the entire human race seeks. In Psalm 35:27 we find recorded that God takes delight in the *shalom (the wholeness, the total well-being)* of His servant. Isaiah 53:5 teaches us that the atonement of Christ included the chastisement necessary to bring us *shalom.* The Greek form is *eirene*, which is a state of rest, quietness, and calmness; an absence of strife; tranquility; a perfect well-being. *Eirene* includes harmonious relationships between God and humanity, individuals and individuals, nations, and families. As you can see, no one definition does justice to this simple, yet complex word. How do we bring this description into the area of peacemaking?

If we are going to be truly happy, we must first access that quality of life that can only come when we make peace with our Creator. This is because it is only through a relationship with Him that we truly find *that* completeness and wholeness that is described by the word *peace.* Before we can be concerned with peacemaking that involves other people's lives, we must take care of our own house and establish a peace relationship with the Lord God. For that person who has not "made their peace with God," there can be no real fullness, wholeness, harmony, etc. We must accept the fact that we are born into enmity towards God and require reconciliation before we can obtain the happiness that Jesus describes in Matthew 5. So, first of all, ***Happy are those who have bridged the gap between themselves and their Maker, thus realizing the well-being that God desires for each one of us.***

The Bible says that since we have been justified by faith, we have peace with God through our Lord Jesus Christ. It also tells us that this peace we have is beyond our comprehension. Look at Romans 5:9-11, *"Since we have now been justified by his blood, how much more shall we be saved from God's wrath through him! For if, when we were God's enemies, we were reconciled to him through the death of his Son, how much more, having been reconciled, shall we be saved through his life! Not only is this so, but we also rejoice in God through our Lord Jesus Christ, through whom we have now received reconciliation."* To continue in applying the term *peacemakers* to our lives, I think we should look at our reconciliation to God and how that affects our mission. Numerous commentaries on the subject of being peacemakers simply address our helping to reduce or prevent arguments between two or more parties. There is an element of that in this, but I think it goes much deeper. If you were in attendance at Abundant Life Church a few weeks ago, you heard me read and address II Corinthians 5:18-20. Forgive the redundancy, as I address these verses here again. *"All this is from God, who . . .* **gave us the ministry of reconciliation:** *. . . And he has committed to us the* **message of reconciliation.** **We are therefore Christ's ambassadors, as though God were making his appeal through us.**" If you want to truly be a peacemaker, assume your ministry of reconciliation and allow God to use you to bring someone to a place of peace with their God. He has given you the ministry of reconciliation, the message of reconciliation, he is making his appeal through you, and therefore you are Christ's ambassador. Do you feel any kind of responsibility yet? **Happy are those who, having been reconciled to their maker, become instruments of mercy as they lead fellow citizens into accessing this peace we are talking about.** Paul began the above passage by saying that we no longer regard anyone from a worldly point of view. The worldly point of view is one of disregard. It is an attitude that says, "What have I got to do with them?" The worldly viewpoint is one that is inward, only concerned with itself and the furthering of its own interests and agenda. Paul says that now we are totally new creations; members of a new species or race of people, and therefore our point of view has changed. We now see through eyes of reconciliation, knowing full well the necessity and blessing of allowing God to forgive us our sins and not count them against us any longer. If you want to be really happy, allow God to use you as the source of this message of reconciliation and observe as a new soul is re-united to their God and thus discovers this peace that you already enjoy. You *peacemaker* you!

Happy are those who are persecuted because of righteousness, for theirs is the kingdom of heaven. Happy are you when people insult you, persecute you and falsely say all kinds of evil against you because of me. Rejoice and be glad, because great is your reward in heaven, for in the same way they persecuted the prophets who were before you. Ah, persecution . . . such a warm subject. I'm sure most of us wake up every day and plead with God to be persecuted sometime during the day. Well, allow me to let you in on a secret. II Timothy 3:12, *"And indeed, all who desire to live godly in Christ Jesus will be persecuted."* Jesus knew full well, as He was instructing the disciples, that eventually they would be reviled by men because of their association with Him. From the beginning people have not understood how believers could be so committed to Christ and His cause. Even today, what people can't understand or explain they attempt to persecute and falsely accuse.

The word *"persecute"* means *to pursue or drive away.* He said "happy are those who are persecuted because of righteousness." Light always exposes darkness. Darkness will do whatever is necessary to not be brought to light. Thus, the natural reaction of one who is controlled by darkness is to pursue or attempt to drive away that which is the source of the light. This is why Jesus follows with a reminder to the disciples that they (and we) are the light of the world. It is also why He describes us as a city set on a hill and reminds us that no one lights a lamp and then hides it. The intention of the lamp is to illuminate everything in the house. *"Let your light shine before men in such a way that they may see your good works"* has new meaning when we view it in the context of what reaction darkness has to light. That is why Jesus confronted Saul on the road to Damascus with the question, "Why are you persecuting Me?" He also teaches Saul, and us as well, a lesson by answering Saul's question of "Who are you?" with the statement, "I am He you are persecuting." Saul had not lifted a finger to Jesus, but had persecuted the followers of Christ. Saul had darkness in his soul, a religious darkness, which caused him to give his life to driving away the Christians who let their light so shine that it made him uncomfortable. I believe that ever since he had held the garments of the men who stoned Stephen, he had trouble sleeping, always seeing the glory of God on Stephen's face and thus, being overcome with guilt because he was in "hearty agreement with putting Stephen to death." Therefore, Paul could confidently state that if we intend to live a godly life, one filled with light, we will definitely be persecuted. If you follow Jesus' instruction and let your light shine, assuredly you will cross paths with someone whom you make uncomfortable, and will thusly attempt to drive you away by pursuit.

How shall we respond to these times of persecution? Well, for a glimpse, look at Proverbs 28:1. *"The wicked flees when no one is pursuing, but the righteous are as bold* (confident*) as a lion."* Paul wrote in his first letter to the church at Corinth, ". . . *when we are reviled, we bless; when we are persecuted, we endure."* In his second letter to the same group, he says, *"But we have this treasure in earthen vessels, that the surpassing greatness of the power may be of God and not from ourselves; . . .* **persecuted, but not forsaken***; struck down, but not destroyed; . . ."* Our response? To endure; to keep getting up when we are proverbially knocked down. And then, after we get up and keep on enduring, Jesus commands us to "*. . . pray for those who persecute you in order that you may be the sons of your Father who is in heaven.*" If we truly understand the source of persecution, rather than taking personal offense and wishing demise on our enemies, we will pray for them. This is born out of our knowledge that their actions are rooted in the fact that the light we reflect is getting a little too close for comfort. It is a little like the oft-quoted Shakespeare line, "Me thinks he protesteth too much."

A final admonition concerning this is found in Peter's first letter. Chapter 3 verses 13-17. "*And who is there to harm you if you prove zealous for what is good? But even if you should suffer for the sake of righteousness, you are blessed (happy). And do not fear their intimidation and do not be troubled, but sanctify Christ as Lord in your hearts, always being ready to make a defense to everyone who asks you to give an account for the hope that is in you, yet with gentleness and reverence; and keep a good conscience so that in the thing in which you are slandered, those who revile your good behavior in Christ may be put to shame. For it is better, if God should will it so, that you suffer for doing what is right rather than for doing what is wrong.*" If we are going to be reviled, we should be careful it is not warranted. Not only do we not want to be responsible for casting tainted light, we also rob the persecutor the opportunity of "seeing the light." In this case we might mistake persecution for the judgment of God.

If you are reviled for the name of Christ, you are blessed (happy), because the Spirit of glory and of God rests upon you. But if anyone suffers as a Christian, let him not feel ashamed, but in that name let him glorify God.

I hope you have been moved, blessed, changed and motivated as you have read these newsletters on Happiness According to Jesus. May the truth in them become more alive to you each and every day. Until next month, hold your head up. You serve an awesome God!!

The Value of Humanity

Someone has described our society as a "valueless" society due to the seeming lack of values among a large portion of our people. While I agree in principle with that statement, I would amend that description to say that we live in a "value misplaced" society. We frequently do place value on certain things, but our priorities and objects of value are often just that, misplaced.

Allow me, as a sidebar, to recommend two books. Tom Brokaw wrote a book a couple of years ago entitled "The Greatest Generation" describing the World War II generation. While I have issues with Mr. Brokaw's political views, I very much enjoyed his helping me to understand the price that group of people paid to allow me the freedom I can enjoy today. The reason I recommend the book here is the value system *that* generation of Americans held onto is sadly disappearing from our fabric of society. Rather than elaborate on that, read the book and you will agree, I'm sure. The second book is a follow up to the first one entitled "The Greatest Generation Speaks." It is a compilation of letters received by Mr. Brokaw from those veterans after the release of the initial publication.

One thing that has been devalued in our current culture is the value of humanity, or the human life. Even though I don't consider myself a senior citizen, (my children would disagree) I never thought I would see, in my relatively short lifetime, the rampant devaluing of the human life at all stages; beginning with abortion of the unborn child all the way to the supposed convenience yielding euthanasia of our elderly citizens, not to mention the equally alarming trend by some in the medical community towards assisted suicide. All this adds up to an attitude that says, "if it is in our way, let's remove it, even if it contains the breath of God."

While I trust no one reading this letter would even consider today some of the things mentioned above, we as Christians may sometimes be guilty of not holding the proper place of value for our fellow human being. The following is a rather long quote from Pastor Jack Hayford on this topic. *"Fallen though he be, man is still deemed by the Almighty to be of inestimable worth. Though incapable of saving himself, man—as creature—represents God's highest and best, made in His image and intended for His glory. In the light of Christ's will to spend His own life for man's redemption, an eternal insight into the worth of man from God's viewpoint is gained. (I Peter 1:18-19) Thus, in our understanding, essential to personal growth and relational development with both God and man is a biblical perspective on the fundamental value of the individual, both in God's sight and in your own. Having created man in His image, God has invested unmeasurable worth in each being. His quest for the redemption of sinful, fallen man is evidence not only of God's love but of His wisdom in working to retrieve that which is of infinite value to Him.*" Do we sometimes drift from the right perspective concerning the awesomeness of God's highest form of creation?

In Luke 10:25-37 we read the story commonly called "The Good Samaritan." It is probably one of the most widely known stories told from Scripture, both in secular and religious settings. Jesus is confronted by an expert in the law with the question, "What must I do to inherit eternal life?" Jesus does something that my wife hates for me to do (does that mean I am like Jesus?); He answers a question with a question. *"How do you read and understand the law?"* Being the expert he was, he replied accurately from Deuteronomy 6:5 and Leviticus 19:18, *"Love the Lord your God with all your heart and with all your soul and with all your strength and with all your mind,"* and, *"Love your neighbor as yourself."* How many of us would do just fine if somehow the sentence from Leviticus hadn't made it in there? Loving our God is one thing, but loving our neighbor is an entirely different muscle to exercise. When Jesus replied that he had answered correctly, the lawyer in this man was revealed. "And who is my neighbor?" Lawyers didn't just recently start looking for legal loopholes. It is inherent in the fallen nature, I think. Jesus at this point begins to tell a story that this gentleman could relate to. He begins to describe a journey from Jerusalem to Jericho. He uses an actual road to draw the law expert into the story emotionally. The road between Jerusalem to Jericho was known in that day as a dangerous path, populated by thieves and muggers. Jesus tells of a man making that trip and was accosted by robbers. They took his clothes, beat him, and left him half-dead.

A priest "happened" to be going down the road. When the man came into view of him, he made sure he passed on the other side of the road. This was due to the ceremonial law that said if a priest touched a dead body he would be disqualified from serving in the temple. Those two weeks were the most important thing in the life of that priest and he wasn't about to let an unfortunate soul derail him. In this instance, he put the temple rituals above the claims of suffering humanity.

The Scripture says that the Levite "came to the place" and saw him. I think this was a close inspection, which was inconclusive as to whether or not this "half-dead" man was "fully dead." He too hurried to the other side of the road. Some have speculated that this servant of the temple, who was involved in the ministry of religious worship, surmised that if the priest passed him by, maybe so should he. In the same vein, the priest might have thought, "I'll leave him for the Levite because he isn't directly involved in the ceremony like I am." Both of these men illustrate that religious work doesn't make the worker righteous. They didn't have the time or the compassion to stop their journey to help this man.

At this point, Jesus could have used any race of people to illustrate His point. He chose to use a Samaritan. Without getting too deep into the history of the Samaritans, suffice it to say they were a mixed race of people who were half Jew. They were so ostracized they separated themselves, built their own temple and created their own religion. No self-respecting Jew would be seen in contact or conversation with a Samaritan, and the opposite was also true. (see John 4) Imagine the jolt that must have went through this lawyer when Jesus said, "*But a _Samaritan_ came where the man was; and when he saw him, he had compassion on him.*" The lawyer saw this man as nothing more than a name to study. The robbers saw him as a nobody, a worthless human being. The priest and Levite saw him as a bother to avoid. But the Samaritan saw him as a neighbor to serve. Jesus purposely made the Samaritan the star of this story. And to this day the term "Samaritan" is synonymous with someone who is willing help a fellow human being. Even to the point that many hospitals have the name "Samaritan" somewhere in their title. The story tells us that the man from Samaria bandaged his wounds, using oil and wine to help begin the healing process. He even went as far as to put him on his own animal and checked him into a nearby inn. When he had to leave because of prior obligations, he gave the innkeeper some money to take care of the man, promising to pay any further balance upon his return.

The expert in the law was undeniably trapped when the question from Jesus resounded in his ears. *"Which of these three do you think was a neighbor to the man who fell into the hands of robbers?"* I don't think it is without notice that the lawyer couldn't say, "The Samaritan." He said, "The one who had mercy on him."

Every day we come into contact with people on the road from here to there. Many times we come upon people who have been stripped of their dignity, self-esteem, and have been left for dead by the enemy of their souls as well as ours. We work with them, go to school with them, and maybe even live next door to them. We are related to people by blood and marriage who we know have been robbed by the one who came for the purpose of stealing, killing, and ultimately destroying them on the road from here to there. What value do you place on that lady sitting next to you on the airplane? How about the fellow parent you have befriended on your son's or daughter's soccer team? Could it be coincidence that we can all identify numerous relationships we have with people that may not be included in our church family? I think not. If we live in the midst of a hurting world of people, and we carry the Bread of Life and the Light of the World in our bosom, what shall we do with such treasure? Will we, as discussed in last month's letter, hide our light under a bushel? Will we reserve the value-laden word of God we have received solely for those in our spiritual family? Or will we, like the Good Samaritan, stop long enough to offer our resources to a wounded and dying soul who just needs someone to care for them? I know these are lots of questions, but questions make us think. Let us follow the example of the Samaritan in responding to those God places in our lives by divine appointment.

How did the Samaritan love this man, and thus, how are we supposed to love our neighbor? It all starts with **compassion**. Well, there is a whole newsletter right there, maybe sometime in the future. Compassion is to "have passion alongside."

This is not a sexual passion, but to be so involved in their lives that we stand beside them, feeling the same passion they have for their hurt and pain. All three of the individuals in this story looked at the wounded man, but only one actually saw him. Only one took time to really see the man and his obvious need; the one who was moved with compassion. This is where true evangelism starts, when God allows us to "feel with" someone in their loss and suffering. If we are going to love our neighbor, we must ask God to give us that kind of compassion for them.

The second thing we see in the life of this Good Samaritan is that he was **willing to get involved**. He never once considered not helping this poor soul because of a possible state of uncleanness. This is a rampant problem in the church today. We have too many religious people who avoid contact with a "sinner" because they are afraid of being labeled "unclean" by their peers. It was not a false accusation when Jesus was described as a "friend of sinners." There is one word the Samaritan didn't avoid, and we must not avoid it if we are going to have personal impact on people's lives along the highway of suffering. That word is risk. There is no such thing as genuine love without risk. This works in all relationships. Without vulnerability you can never experience the full effect of loving and being loved. If we shield ourselves from hurt, we also shield ourselves from love. As we are confronted with people who are in need of some of our oil and wine, we must be willing to go beyond any religious limitations and reach our hand out to them.

This topic seems to be coming up a lot lately; but, the third way the Good Samaritan displayed love for the wounded man was he **showed him mercy**. We learned two newsletters ago that mercy is *active compassion*. It isn't enough that we "feel their pain" (sorry, it seemed to fit), we must also make our animal and other resources available to bring our object of mercy to healing. In this way, we make our compassion an active reality. James, the brother of our Lord, must have had this story in mind when he wrote, "*What good is it, my brothers, if a man claims to have faith but has no deeds? Can such faith save him? Suppose a brother or sister is without clothes and daily food. If one of you says to him, 'Go, I wish you well; keep warm and well fed,' but does nothing about his physical needs, what good is it?*" We must show that we care, not just say so.

The last approach I see in this passage is that the Samaritan **stopped** to help this man, **regardless of the cost**. He was obviously on his way somewhere important, but was willing to postpone his schedule for two days so he could stay with this injured man to make sure he would be okay. What do we think when we know that distressed soul needs us to deviate from our plans and offer assistance? What happens when that lady at work who has been having marital problems needs to talk to you, and you don't have time because it would inconvenience you away from your important schedule? When we cross paths with someone who has been robbed and stripped, are we willing to pay the cost necessary to get them to a healthy place? We must value that human life as God does.

From this story, we learn three final things that we can apply to our lives. *First*, the secret to loving humanity is not found in religion or religious activities. In fact, religious activities will anesthetize us to the real need. *Second*, it is not found in responsibility. True love isn't borne out of simple obligation. We might go through the motion, but ultimately the recipient of our actions will be robbed of true, Christ-like love if it is due simply to a sense of obligation. *Third*, true love develops out of a relationship. This is why I am so high on lifestyle evangelism. The greatest evangelistic impact we will have is going to be upon those with whom we have developed relationships of some kind. Wherever we find ourselves on a regular basis, there we will find people with whom God has crossed our paths for a divine purpose. Keep your spiritual eyes and ears peeled and watch for that soul lying beside the road in need of a compassion-filled Good Samaritan to stop and bring them to a place of healing. Don't cross to the other side of the road and place other concerns above what is facing you.

Our value of humanity will determine how we approach one another and how sensitive we are to those divine appointments the Father places along our path. Let us pray to God that He will allow us to see humanity through His eyes. Then, I am confident our response will be similar to His.

The Celebration of Light

I was walking through a department store in late October, and became angry when I saw the Christmas items already out on the shelf and in the aisles. It was bad enough they had Halloween items on display, yet it was even more disturbing to see Christmas decorations and promotions alongside. Late October! I suppose it angers me a little more each year how our culture has so commercialized the Christmas event that it detracts a little from the enjoyment of this time of year. This is one of the reasons I so enjoy Thanksgiving and the harvest festival time of year so much. May I whisper something in your ear? Promise not to tell Wall Street this secret? (They have never figured out how to commercialize Thanksgiving.) When was the last time you saw Thanksgiving paraphernalia displayed before the end of October?

Well, my campaign is to take back Christmas from the Wall Street racketeers and luxuriate in what should be the most joyful time of year. I know some feel that Christmas is a pagan holiday and we shouldn't participate in this celebration anyway. That kind of thinking will force you and me to rename the days of the week and disregard the calendars on our walls. Many of the days of the week and months of the year were named after pagan gods and gods of Greek mythology. I suggest we take the celebration of the birth of our Lord back *from* whomever has captured it and perverted the true meaning.

It is entirely possible, although I do not portray myself to be an expert in these matters, that Jesus was born sometime in the spring of the year, rather than the winter as we celebrate. Am I suggesting we shift our celebration to the spring? Certainly not. I don't think <u>when</u> we celebrate the revealing of "God with us" is necessarily as important as the fact that we <u>do,</u> in fact, set aside a time of focusing on this momentous time in history. And so, since the entire world chooses December as this time, we join with them and honor the coming of our Lord Jesus Christ.

At the time of Christ's birth the world was in such a state of chaos, sickness, and spiritual darkness that Brother Charles Simpson once compared it to the condition of the earth in Genesis 1:2. The Scripture tells us that the earth was without form and was an empty waste. We are also told that darkness was upon the face of the earth. When Jesus was born, the society he arrived in was so corrupt, the darkness it held could indeed be compared to the darkness and chaos described in

Genesis. We simply need to look no further than King Herod's reaction to the news of the birth of the "king of the Jews," and his violent act of destroying all the male children under two years of age, and surely the words darkness and disorder come to mind. As in Genesis when God said, "Let there be light," He repeated Himself when He sent the light of the world to live among us. In sending Jesus in the form of a human to redeem the human race, God was simply saying, "Let there be light where there is presently darkness and let that light be not temporary, but it shall be an eternal illumination." I would like to submit to you that *Christmas is a celebration of light entering the world and shining on its chaos and darkness*.

If we examine the 7th, 8th, and 9th chapters of Isaiah, we can see how it was prophesied that Jesus would come to us as the Light of the world. In chapter 7 we find Ahaz, King of Judah, is mortally afraid of the threatening trio of King Rezin of Aram, Pekah, king of Israel, and Ephraim. A parallel passage in II Kings 16 tells us that Ahaz sought help from the king of Assyria. The Lord scolds Ahaz for his lack of trust in the Lord with this statement. *"If you do not stand firm in your faith, you will not stand at all."* He says through Isaiah that He will give Ahaz a sign as to the source of his redemption and protection. God proclaims *"the virgin will be with child and will give birth to a son, and will call him*

Immanuel." No matter what difficulty we may face, God is always reminding us that He has taken up permanent residence "with us." Over in chapter 8 Isaiah says that God "with His strong hand upon me" warns him not to follow the way of this unbelieving people. Verses 12-14 say it this way; *"Do not call conspiracy everything that these people call conspiracy; do not fear what they fear, and do not dread it. The Lord Almighty is the one you are to regard as holy, he is the one you are to fear, He is the one you are to dread, and He will be a sanctuary."* Later in the same chapter Isaiah says instead of consulting mediums and spiritists, we should inquire of our God for our deliverance and strength. He prophesies that people will become distressed and hungry roaming throughout the land until they are so famished they will look to the heavens and begin to curse God. Verse 22 says, *"Then they will look toward the earth and see only distress and darkness and fearful gloom, and they will be thrust into utter darkness."*

Faint not, but only look to verse 1 of chapter 9. *"Nevertheless, there will be no more gloom for those who were in distress."* God chooses to not leave us in our distress, neither as a people nor as a nation. He is always illuminating our path, shining His light on that which seeks to hinder us from following the path which grows brighter with each step. He continues on in verse 2 of chapter 9 by saying, *"The people walking in darkness have seen a great light; on those living in the land of the shadow of death a light has dawned . . . For to us a child is born, to us a Son is given, and the government will be on His shoulders. And He will be called Wonderful Counselor, Mighty God, Everlasting Father, Prince of Peace. Of the increase of His government and peace there will be no end."*

Jesus is presented to us as the source of light entering into this world. People walking in darkness have seen a great light, because a child has been born to us, to whom the government of all God's kingdom has been conferred. In this season of the year, we are celebrating the fact that Jesus revealed righteousness to a confused and oppressed society. The culture He was born into was corrupted by its religion and oppressed by the Roman military and political power. When Jesus said that He came not to bring peace, but rather division, He was referring to the fact that He would naturally separate darkness from light. When the Son of God is allowed into the place of darkness, He so illuminates His surroundings that people feel bigger than their circumstances, and they rejoice with an increased joy.

John said of Jesus that He was the *"true light that gives light to every man who comes into the world."* Jesus said of Himself, *"I am the light of the world. Whoever follows me will never walk in darkness, but will have the light of life."*

What does light do? First of all, light illuminates everything in the area. In illuminating, light exposes that which may have been hidden in the darkness. As a result of exposing and illuminating, which enables the fruit of darkness to be dealt with, light also gives life to us. Jesus said we would have the "light of life." It's the things hidden in darkness that will destroy us. When those things are brought into the light, salvation from their bondage is not far away.

What does darkness do? It seduces us into hiding. Darkness willingly hides those things that will intentionally handicap us from achieving God's ultimate purpose for us. Darkness also gives us a false sense of well being. We think if it is not exposed, it has no impact on our lives. That's sort of like the idea that if it can't be seen, maybe it isn't really there. Another thing darkness will do to us is to create a fear due to the unknown. There is something about the unknown that naturally causes us trepidation at the very least. When we think of darkness, we not only think of fear, but it is the darkness of the night that is most populated with criminal activities. There is a spiritual reason that most crimes are committed at night. Darkness gives us a false sense of security. It is cold and chilling.

On the other hand, light brings us peace, confidence, and warmth. When everything is exposed, we walk in truth. And the knowledge of that truth will cause you and me to walk in freedom.

Is it possible we have darkness in our land today? Is it possible the same Spirit that hovered over the darkness in Genesis 1 is the same Spirit that hovered over and overshadowed the Virgin Mary, causing the light of the world to be born? The obvious answer to both questions is yes. In addition, the same Spirit that hovered over the earth and the Virgin Mary still broods over the darkness we have in our world today. Everywhere we declare the living word of God, the Holy Spirit proceeds separating light from darkness. Whenever the light shows up on the scene, darkness retreats.

Jesus said, "I am the Light of the world." He said to the disciples in another place, "You are the light of the world." Was Jesus confused? I think not. When the moon receives the light of the sun, it has no choice other than to shine that light so all can see. We are the recipients of the light that comes from the Savior, and naturally reflect that light to those around us. We are exhorted to let our light shine before men, that they may see our good deeds and praise our Father in heaven. While I have not the space to deal with it here, there is even the element of God causing the light in us to break the blindness of unbelievers, so they can see the light of the gospel.

So there you have it, a reason to celebrate beyond Hallmark and Wal-Mart. I see no problem with the giving and receiving of gifts in this season. The problem I see is when we become so consumed with those things, we lose sight of the real reason to celebrate; The Celebration of Light.

Jesus said, *"This is the verdict: Light has come into the world, but men loved darkness instead of light because their deeds were evil. Everyone who does evil hates the light, and will not come into the light for fear that his deeds will be exposed. But whoever lives by the truth comes into the light, so that it may be seen plainly that what he has done has been done through God."*

ACKNOWLEDGEMENTS

I would be remiss if I did not acknowledge those who have contributed to my being able to undertake such an endeavor. I certainly cannot identify everyone who has helped or inspired me over the years, but I will make a valiant attempt at naming a few.

First of all, I must mention the inspiration for such a newsletter. Between the late 60's and the middle 80's, there was a magazine published called <u>New Wine Magazine</u> which featured the writings of Charles Simpson, Bob Mumford, Derek Prince, Don Basham, Ern Baxter, and many others. It was a magazine that came each month chock full of bible teaching in written form; in some ways, a sermon in writing. I looked forward each month to the <u>New Wine</u> coming in because it was always rich with instruction from the Scripture. When I began to write the Kernels of Truth, the articles in the former magazine were not only my model, but my inspiration as well.

I must thank my mother, Betty Grainger, who undertook the daunting task of raising three sons in the ways of God in the years before my father came to become a believer in Christ. Without that foundation and consistency in the church, I am sure my life would have turned out much differently, and mostly not good. Her success can be measured in the fact that all three of us are walking in the way of Christ and are intricately involved in our respective churches.

I must recognize Rob Shearer and Green Leaf Publishing. Rob has greatly assisted in getting this book to print and with some editing of the book. I am not sure that I could have done this without the help of Rob.

In addition, I would like to thank Kelly Pody for poring over this manuscript and applying her "teaching" skills to correcting and suggesting. She has been a valuable resource and I thank her.

Also, I would like to thank Steve Tyrrell for the cover design and layout. It looks better than I could have ever imagined. Steve sacrificed greatly on this project to make it happen, so if you have graphic or communications needs, please consider Tyrrell Graphics. The contact information can be found opposite the title page at the beginning of the book.

I would also like to thank Curtis Forman who served as my pastor for 16 years, mostly during the developmental years of my life and ministry. Curtis was always that steadying and stable force in my life as I found my way as a young pastor. Much of the content of the Kernels of Truth was born out of our relationship and his instruction. He remains a close friend of mine today.

I couldn't even begin to think about having done this for these many years without the faithfulness and love of my beautiful wife, Anne. She has always been my biggest fan and loving critic. As of this writing, we have been married for over 37 years. When I think of all she has had to endure during that time, I surmise that sainthood is looming somewhere in her future. And, in addition to being my helpmate and soul mate, Anne has been my faithful proofreader for each issue of Kernels of Truth. I could not have done this without her.

Lastly, but certainly not least, I must acknowledge my Lord God, the Father of all. The only reason I have been able to publish this newsletter through the years, and continue to do so now, is due to a gift from the Father of lights to be able to write. The Scripture teaches us that "*Every good and perfect gift comes down from the Father of lights.*" The ability for me to sit down to the computer each month and produce another teaching from the Bible can only be accomplished because of the Lord distributing to me a gift to do so. I am thankful and bewildered by such a gift. But, nevertheless, I continue to write the Kernels of Truth for the purpose of bringing glory to the Most High God.

Made in the USA
Charleston, SC
05 April 2011